Dear T

Your unconditional support, & gentle guiding by example helped light the way for this book to come forth! Thank you!

With Much
Peace & Love, Janice

YOUR INDELIBLE WORTH

Published by Lisa Hagan Books 2022

www.lisahaganbooks.com

Copyright © Janine Miller-DeLany 2022

ISBN: 978-1-945962-45-5

All Rights Reserved. No part of this publication may be reproduced, stored in a retrieval system, or transmitted in any form, or by any means, electronic, mechanical, photocopying, recording or otherwise without the prior permission in writing of the copyright holders, nor be otherwise circulated in any form or binding or cover other than in which it is published and without a similar condition being imposed on the subsequent publisher.

Cover photography: Frank McKenna http://blog.frankiefoto.com/

Cover design and interior layout by Simon Hartshorne

Your Indelible Worth

A Spiritual Journey Dedicated
to Your Highest Self

JANINE MILLER-DELANY

Contents

Foreword 7

Introduction 11

How These Messages of Love Came to Be 17

How to Use This Personal Guide to Remembering 21

LESSON ONE: *Our Bond Is Unbreakable* 25

LESSON TWO: *I Am Ever Your Guide* 45

LESSON THREE: *Trust Wholly in Me* 65

LESSON FOUR: *My Will for You Is Happiness* 83

LESSON FIVE: *The Power of Surrender* 99

LESSON SIX: *The Power of Acceptance* 119

LESSON SEVEN: *Return to Your Natural State* 135

LESSON EIGHT: *You Are My Guiltless Child* 153

LESSON NINE: *You Are Already Home, Complete in Me* 173

LESSON TEN: *Release the Illusion of Separation*..................191

LESSON ELEVEN: *In Our Union is All Power*..................209

LESSON TWELVE: *Your Worth Is Indelible*......................227

Exercises for Emotional Clearing and Absorbing Truth......................249

    #1 *A Daily Practice in Blissful Trust*......................250

    #2 *Clearing Blocks with The Tree of Judgment*............................253

    #3 *Absorbing Love with the Tree of Compassion*............................256

    #4 *Integrating Your Truth*..260

    #5 *Soaking into your Natural State with Love Itself (in italics)*...............262

    #6 *Absorbing Gratitude*...264

    #7 *Making Space for Balance and Rest*...................................265

FOR MY BELOVED
JERE MICHAEL
who helps me stay ever attuned
to the current of pure love

Foreword

The very fact that you are looking at this book, reading these words, is a sure sign that you are ready to leap into the truth of your Self. You have been led here by your true Self, your greatest friend and infallible guide. You are ready to move, gently, freely, without the impediment of expectations, into your magnificence.

Because you have come this far in your spiritual quest—to the threshold of this book—turning back is no longer possible. You might delay the inevitable for a little while, perhaps, but your beautiful destiny is in sight, or more accurately said, it's within *feel*. And that *feel* is irresistible because it is what you are: Love Itself.

Love cannot be taught. It cannot be learned. *Your Indelible Worth* is not another learning tool. But if you take it in, this book will be a powerful presence in your life. Through it, the truth of your Self, which is love, will be felt, recognized, imbibed, accepted, and allowed to rule.

Let it.

The spiritual quest is unlike any other. There's an ancient Chinese phrase, "Wu wei," literally meaning "effortless action." Wu wei describes a state of being in harmony with What Is. In *Your Indelible Worth* Janine frequently refers to the necessity of effortlessness. Effortlessness is a concept so contrary to modern Western society that it begs for a little explaining. Does "effortlessness" suggest that we be couch potatoes before the omnipresent electronic screen? No. Does it suggest that spiritual attainment is easy? Not necessarily.

Jesus addresses the question of effortlessness as it relates to his masterpiece, *A Course of Love*. There he said:

> The seeming lack of difficulty in this Course is where its difficulty lies. To give up difficulty for ease is more than some egos are willing to accept. To give up effort for receptivity is more than some can accept. Why? Because it is too difficult. It goes against all you have learned and the nature of the reality in which the mind has functioned. In turning to the heart we seek to bypass this difficulty as much as possible . . .

Here, too, *Your Indelible Worth* goes against the patterns of life as you have learned them to be, and turns to the heart—that is, to your soul, the center of your Self—to bypass the habitual objections of the mind. The extent to which the critical mind can be set aside is the extent to which *Your Indelible Worth* will be beneficial.

Your Indelible Worth is filled with messages that came to Janine's receptive heart-mind over the past decades from "Love Itself"—another name for the Divine Within, or God. If you allow them, these messages can be akin to being tenderly held, such as: *I can rest on the current of your love for me.*

Sometimes Love Itself is intimately physical:

My body softens, the tension drains out in tears with no words to speak
as comfort and love from beyond this manifested world
soak into my tired muscles strained from years of trying too hard.
I breathe in a new breath, now the breath I share with Love Itself.

Sometimes Love Itself can be challenging:

> *Do you understand that when you doubt yourself, you question Me?*

And again:

> *If you could trust in the pure love that you are,
> then would you see you need nothing.*

Your Indelible Worth is part of a growing wave in which seemingly separate humans are coming into direct relationships with God. It is happening more so than ever before in human history. Janine is the receiver, but so are you. The words in this book come to you, dear reader, from your own divine voice, the voice of your true consciousness. Your Being is speaking to you.

Your own Being is asking, "How is my heart? How well am I keeping this blessed heart? What dwells there, fear or love?" Ever so gently, this message from your own soul will allow your reserved, fearful self to give way to knowing, to certainty, to trust, to love.

The messages and exercises in *Your Indelible Worth* are both sweet and powerful. They will not throw you panic-stricken into Oneness, but tenderly allow you to experience it. Go forth in peace and confidence into this book.

Glenn Hovemann
Editor, Miracles Magazine
Publisher, Take Heart Publications,
publisher of *A Course of Love* and the
seven-volume series, *Choose Only Love*

Introduction

We endeavor to know the depth of our own worth. We have all asked ourselves, what is my worth, why am I here, and what is my purpose?

For most of us, the internal struggle with the truth of our innate worth shows up in a multitude of ways. Often, we end up trying too hard to earn or prove our worth, and that trying tends to complicate things even more. In this book, I describe how we tend to complicate things and assist you with solutions that have worked for my clients and for me. It may be those subconscious efforts to earn your worth cause you to miss out on many of the simple moments of happiness, peace, and just enjoying this ride of life in the way your soul, deep down, knows it's meant to be.

It has never been more evident in our stressful lifestyles and daily news that most of humanity struggles to remember who we are. This book will remind you who you really are and how deeply you are loved, *exactly* as you are.

As you journey with me along this path, you will find both an invitation and an opening to return to your natural state. You are no longer bound by self-doubt, fear, pressure, expectations, or any limitations in that state. Instead, in your natural state, you get to return to the childlike joy, freedom, and wonder that existed before the cares and messages of the world took their grip on you. In your natural state, you live again as the fullest expression of yourself, ever-expanding, growing, and creating in perfect alignment with your Source within you.

When we learn to look with greater love upon ourselves, we will then be able to love and accept others. Ask yourself, however, how can you give the best of yourself if you do not first remember the truth of who you are and what you have to give?

I have not met a person in my counseling office whose core struggle does not always return to a question of innate worth. You may not be able to see it yet, but when you do have that small willingness to acknowledge it, you will have opened yourself up to healing and limitless joy and freedom.

The Messages of Love included here in this book speak to the core of this struggle in a way no therapist can. The healing love within these Messages resonates to the very center of one's being. There is a memory that is called upon and a door within the heart that begins to open as you allow yourself to just receive the deep love within.

No matter which road you have traveled or what has led you here, you will find peace, hope, and even excitement in a new and refreshing way. For the Voice within you is speaking and is anxious to meet you here. So many of us have been flailing about, lost in a churning sea of chaos and uncertainty. The more we hone in on the trying or news watching or worrying, the more helpless we feel. Essentially, Love Itself is throwing all of us a lifeline.

In sharing some of my own personal stories, I hope you feel like you are walking this journey with a trusted friend. I have found this to be a unique opportunity to awaken to your indelible worth through the eyes of Divine Love and in so doing, discover the bliss of feeling complete and free, precisely as you were created. And that, my friend, gives you new eyes to see that you get to be the creator of your own life story.

Introduction

A Little More About Me

I was raised in Columbus, Ohio, and shortly after college, I moved to the little town of Upper Sandusky, Ohio. It only took a few years of living in a small Midwest town and sharing in church study groups to realize how fortunate I was to be raised in a church where I was taught that God is love and that is all. I've learned through others' stories over the years that is not often the case. I never experienced the teachings of a God who is punishing or judging. The God I grew up knowing loves all and includes all, no exceptions. The message I first learned about sin was from my mother, and that was simply that sin is what it feels like to be apart from God. I felt that I had a leg up in the self-esteem category regarding religion as I never doubted my own innate goodness from the church's perspective. I was, however, exposed to painful experiences, even trauma that cast doubt upon that. I've had my share of health issues and faced Cancer, and treatments in my early 20s. A unique blend of life challenges and gifts caused me to deepen my search for peace and a sense of the presence of Divine Love at a very early age.

I am grateful that I never had a strong need to defend my faith and grew up with an openness to all religions and beliefs. For me, God is in all and can express through all. I explain this because you will find that I describe Divine Love in many ways with no clear attachment to any name. Many people have negative experiences with different names we give to that which is the great I Am. So, for me, I interchange the names easily. God, Divine Love, Source, Creator, and Love Itself are all names I may use to describe what has become an incredibly personal relationship with that which I really can't ultimately name. As I'm coming to realize that there is a Oneness to all that is, I then see that my efforts to individualize Divine Love with a name are just my attempts to see Love Itself through the eyes of my human form and perception. Maybe, Love

Itself is not actually one being high in the sky. Perhaps the Source of All Love is everywhere all the time, even within me, and expressed through me. Jesus, for me, was God communicating through a human form to help us "get it" and understand how deeply we are loved and even the nature of the universe. I believe Divine Love used and continues to use many people to express and teach the depth of such love.

Throughout the writings of these Messages of Love, I've distinguished 12 Lessons that Love Itself has illuminated for me. In stepping back to look at the broader picture, I see that the more I grasp my own worth through the eyes of Divine Love, the more I open myself to align with and therefore receive the abundant gifts of life meant for all of us. I'm finding that I truly am the creator of my own life experience. This is the most wonderfully freeing and exciting part of all of it. I love it when others see and experience the thrill of this as well. This is the best part of getting to walk with others on this journey. We genuinely inspire each other as we witness and experience this awakening within ourselves and each other.

Within this book, you will find that each chapter addresses one of these 12 Lessons. With each lesson, I share one or more of my own personal reflections of the teaching, 10 daily Messages of Love, along with guided reflecting prompts. Additionally, there is a meditation at the end of each chapter, which you may find helpful to repeat or carry with you throughout your month. I'd like to challenge you to convert these meditations into personal affirmations and memorize the ones that speak most powerfully to you. In repetition, we rewrite neural pathways within the brain and thus can shift negative thinking patterns to those more aligned with the inner truth of our indelible worth. Finally, following the 12 Lessons, you'll find seven Exercises for Emotional Clearing and Absorbing Truth to help you push through the emotional blocks that might get in the way and more fully absorb the truth within the Messages.

Additionally, allowing these Messages of Love to sink in daily can even create a "felt sense" of knowing or clarity which will generate new thinking and feeling patterns. The unique combination will free you to live your life as your fullest and limitless version of yourself instead of recycling old thinking/feeling patterns that keep you stuck in the same life situations. I encourage you to find your own separate journal to write your reflections and responses to the journaling prompts. You can visit the Hearts Way Etsy store if you would like to explore a few options I have created.

Permitting yourself to acknowledge and release the emotional blocks along this journey will help propel you forward. Being a counselor has given me access to many tricks of the trade that enabled me to push through my own personal blocks...and I've had many! I will be doing my best to demonstrate some of those techniques to you and, when needed, point you to the resources that helped me the most. This is where the Deeper Emotional Work exercises come in. As a matter of fact, before you begin anything, you might want to skip first to the Emotional Clearing Exercise entitled, The Tree of Judgment. This, combined with The Tree of Compassion is an excellent tool that you may decide to regularly use any time you feel an emotional block or just want a process for further absorbing the Message of Love. Whenever I feel heavy or stuck, I find relief in working both exercises together. Always follow the Tree of Judgment with the Tree of Compassion. They are meant to be used together if you feel an emotional block.

How These Messages of Love Came to Be

In the Spring of 2009, I was walking home from a church service entitled, "Stations of the Cross" with my husband, Jere. It was the week of Easter, and this service was experiential in that it helped participants more fully realize what Jesus' journey to the cross may have felt like for him. As we walked home contemplating the experience, Jere looked to me with a particular question that was perplexing him. He said, "What I don't understand is why Jesus had to die such a *painful* death? Do you know?" Having no response, I could only shake my head and ponder the same question that baffled me as well.

It was a quiet and relaxing early Spring Day so we both decided to take a nap upon our return home. We rested peacefully on the soft bed of our Ohio home and drifted off to sleep. What happened next would awe and perplex me for many years to come. I was awakened to an experience in which I was present to witness Jesus carrying the cross up a hill on a dirt path. I felt myself amongst a crowd of people standing alongside the path jeering and yelling. I witnessed the entire event feeling as if I was right there, standing amongst the crowd, watching as Jesus painstakingly stepped with the weight of the cross on his back. As He passed before me, I heard a voice speak to me as clearly as if it were right next to me. It said, "He had to die such a painful death so that my people would know there is nothing so terrible that they ever could do to me that would keep me from loving them. He had to die such a painful death so that you would know there is *nothing* that could keep me from loving you." And then the voice repeated three times, "Tell them how much I love them. Tell them how much I love them. Tell them how much I love them."

As I lay mesmerized in the experience and watching Jesus move past me, I maintained an awareness that Jere was lying in bed bedside me. In amazement, I noted to him that I now had the answer to his question. I began to repeat to Jere exactly the words as I heard them although I was uncertain that he was even awake.

Gradually I was pulled out of the vision by the feeling of warmth on my face and body. As I came fully into the present moment, the sun spilled in through our bedroom window and glowed more brightly than I had ever felt before. It seemed to illuminate the entire space around us. I laid there soaking in the sun and felt the wetness of a tear trickle down my face as I tried to absorb the magnitude of the moment.

I laid in awe and shock awhile, trying to grasp the experience and the reality that it seemed God himself had just spoken directly to me. As the days passed, the thrill of this reality that the Creator of the Universe had spoken directly to me, turned to a deep, and longing question of, "How?" I found myself asking, "I get that you want me to tell people how much you love them, but how? Do I write it? Speak it? Is there some special way I should go about this?"

I made my best efforts through counseling work, retreats, and speaking engagements, however, I never really felt I was quite meeting the magnitude of the calling that had so clearly been delegated to me. It was not until January of 2019 that a friend introduced me to the teachings of Abraham Hicks. Now I was quite familiar with the concepts of The Law of Attraction as I had already published a guided journal centered on this law and the teachings of Jesus as I had found them to be one in the same. I found Abraham's teachings to be extremely uplifting and validating.

What struck me most pointedly was Esther's story of how Abraham came to speak through her. Esther's experience resonated

How These Messages of Love Came to Be

with my deep, inner knowing that Divine Love most likely had more to say to me and had, in fact, already communicated so clearly to me.

I began to follow Abraham's advice and recommitted to meditating daily for 20 to 40 minutes. This time, I began with a clear intention to hear what God would have me hear and know what God would have me know. What rapidly followed most days of meditation were messages that felt like they were spoken directly to me in response to whatever state I found myself to be in, at the moment. They responded directly to every struggle I was facing and gave me clarity beyond my normal comprehension. These messages came to flow as an outpouring of love, support, and encouragement from Love Itself. The words flowed quickly and easily. I simply waited in meditation until I felt words forming and was compelled to pick up my pen and write. It soon dawned on me that I had finally allowed myself to receive the answer to my burning question, "How do you want me to tell them?" This is how this book came to be.

These Messages of Love are clearly an in-depth declaration of how deeply we are loved. We are indeed so much more alike than we are different and in my years of counseling, I've not met with one person who wouldn't greatly benefit from hearing even a piece of what is conveyed. Very fortunate are those of us who've come upon them and are absorbing them into our hearts. Those of us who thus far have gotten to hear them have found them to be life changing. I believe you will too.

While there were no visions that came with these messages this time, there have come amusing ironies as I've come to see how badly I still need to hear these messages of love as much as anyone. I often must return to acceptance that these words could not possibly be of my own conscious writing since they were and remain answers to my own deepest questions and struggles. My husband, Jere, still laughs when I remark at the insanity of my own personal ego messages despite being the receiver of such remarkable peace and love. To this day, when I read any one of these messages, they feel surprising and new each time. I marvel at how I could write such wisdom and still read each anew as if written by someone else. I am now accepting more fully; it truly is someone else. It is Love Itself.

This morning I was awakened at 5am with the first line of this introduction repeating itself and a strong compulsion to write. I got up in a daze, turned on my light, shocked to see the time, shuffled to the kitchen, bewildered at why I was up so early when I had most definitely planned to sleep in. I knew I was being summoned to begin writing. Thank goodness God is patiently persistent as I have found myself being led through much resistance and fear to allow this book to unfold. And you will soon come to see, Love Itself will gladly do the same for you. For these messages of love are meant for all of us.

❊ ❊ ❊

Within these pages may you come to
know Love Itself within you.

May you thus *remember* who you are.

And in remembering, may you *awaken* to your
power in union with Love Itself.

Thus, may you discover your life is without limits.

❊ ❊ ❊

How to Use This Personal Guide to Remembering

1) Start by reading the personal reflection at the beginning of each of the 12 lessons to help yourself grasp the concept within the lesson and remember you are not alone. I've included quotes from A Course In Miracles and A Course of Love at the beginning of each of my reflections, simply because the love and guidance within has been incredibly healing and transformative for me for the past 20 years. I want to share some of that with all of you.

....

The 10 Messages of Love and writing prompts within each lesson are meant to be absorbed one day at a time, over the course of ten days.

....

2) Next, take 5 to 15 minutes to sit in meditation before reading each daily Message of Love from Love Itself. Meditation helps to clear the body and mind of all the blocks and resistance that would get in the way of being able to hear and feel what Divine Love is longing to share with you. Without meditation, the Message of Love may just feel like words and get stuck in the analyzing mind. Meditation, the stillness of mind and release of the sense of body, frees you to absorb the truth of the Messages. You may begin in silence, focusing on your breath or you may want to follow a guided meditation from a meditation app or teacher.

You can find a simple meditation under **Step 1** of **The COMMA Meditation Journey** on the Journeys Page of my website, the-heartsway.org. **The COMMA Meditation Journey** is also on my podcast, "Divine Chaos: Spiritual Awakenings, Psychotherapy, & The Jacked-Up Journey of Our Life". This is the process given to me over several months by Love Itself. It has been my most direct practice that brings me into a state of full union with Love Itself. One or both together would be very helpful prior to reading each daily Message of Love.

3) Read the daily Message of Love (in italics) slowly. Let the compassion and care of the message sink into your heart and muscles. You might read it once in silence and then another time out loud. See if it soaks in a little deeper with a second reading Try not to overthink or analyze. This is a time to just receive the love, support, and guidance there for you. If there is something you don't yet get, or understand, don't worry about it. Let Divine Love reveal its meaning to you over time. Trust it will come. (You may also choose to listen to the audio version of this book in tandem with this hard copy so that you can hear and absorb these Messages with their inflections and tone. This will create a more powerful absorbing of the depth within these Messages of Love.)

4) Turn to the Deeper Emotional Work exercises at the back of this book any time you are feeling blocked, heavy or if you want a tool to help you absorb the messages more fully. You might find that one resonates or is more helpful than another for you. Use any of them as often as you can or whenever you find yourself needing a little more help to find your peaceful space of truth within. Be careful to follow and read the guidance within them slowly and carefully. If you read or work too fast, without absorbing the process, you may miss much or all the benefits.

5) Consider inviting your friend or a life partner to share and explore your reflections together. Processing your experiences out loud with another or even in a small group may help you deepen your awareness, further integrate the lessons, release ego-messaging, and experience Love's presence in a new way.

※ ※ ※

Take care to make as much time for yourself as you can. You're worth it! But don't judge yourself if you miss a day or don't take as much time as you'd like.

There are 10 Messages of Love within each Lesson, which I encourage you to reread and absorb throughout the month. If you have time to repeat each message on two or three different days, then you will utilize the benefit of repetition to reshape your neural pathways and establish new thinking patterns. Approach all of this with kindness and compassion for yourself. Divine Love wants you to be happy, free, and realize how deeply you are loved!

I look forward to walking with you on this meditative and experiential journey to remembering who you are. Let yourself feel deeply and expand your insight on these pages! Find your own special journal in which you can reflect, color, explore, dream, challenge, and come to believe in your unquestionable, innate worth! As you approach the reflective exercises, remember, there is no right or wrong, good or bad here. There is only love, acceptance, and compassion! All you truly need is an open willingness to hear what Love Itself would have you hear and remember what you have forgotten. Love Itself will take care of the rest.

LESSON ONE:

Our Bond Is Unbreakable

I had a dream.
I stood barefoot, disheveled upon my back deck,
having stepped outside with my two beagles
by my side, in the early evening air.
Peering out upon our yard with five-foot-high
fencing surrounding our sacred space,
we froze in terror as three massive beasts came
one by one to our gate and tried to enter.
I yelled, terrified as adrenaline pumped through my veins.
My dogs barked with a fear none of us had ever
known. All of us trembling, paralyzed by sight.
The beasts left slowly then, one by one, as they
had come, for they could not enter.
Next, there came a circling line, standing side by side,
of great and sturdy stallions and beautiful buffalo.
Majestic, they stood shoulder to shoulder along
our tall fence surrounding our country yard.
In unison, they took one mighty step forward,
and we felt the vibration move within us.
The large fence dropped beneath their feet with no effort at all.
Power, beauty, awe, and wonder stood before us.
No fear overcame us this time.
Instead, a soothing balm of protection steadied
us as if a distant memory had returned.
I recognized then, the great powers of
love from beyond my barriers,
breaking into the reality I thought I knew,
displaying their grandeur and their might.
And I know now, deep in my memory, I have nothing to fear.
A power of love far grander than my own is here
replacing the limited view of my perception
and breaking me free.
Beyond all limits I will go.

Lesson One: Our Bond Is Unbreakable

"I am surrounded by the Love of God. Father, You stand before me and behind, beside me, in the place I see myself, and everywhere I go. You are in all the things I look upon, the sounds I hear, and every hand that reaches for my own. In You time disappears and place becomes a meaningless belief. For what surrounds Your Son and keeps him safe is Love Itself."
~**A Course in Miracles, OrEd.WkBk.264.1**

"Your choice to separate from God is but a separation from your own Self, and this is truly the separation that needs to be healed to return you to God."
~**A Course Of Love C:17.2**

It was morning in early June, and I'd just enjoyed a peaceful meditation while sitting in the sunshine on my back deck. At this point, I'd opened a bit of a dialogue with God in preparation for the yard work awaiting me. I had been contemplating how long I should wait to see if one of my favorite rose bushes was going to show signs of life after the frigid Ohio winter. I had found a tiny sprout of green at the base, but overall, it looked like it could be a very long time before it would come back to life. I had received an inner knowing that it would, in fact, survive, and had pleaded with my husband to give it another week or two to rebirth itself. I must admit, it felt a bit like a metaphor for my own life, and I really wanted to give it a chance. A few weeks had passed. I was impatient to see roses where all that appeared were dry, hollow branches…barring the tiny speck of green at the very bottom.

I was feeling invigorated and inspired by my meditation and decided to give myself permission to dig it up and plant a new one, despite my inner knowing that it was not wholly dead. Jere, my husband, had gone to work his nursing shift at 6 am, and so I prepared myself to muscle it out alone as I headed out with our most durable shovel and heavy work gloves. I knew it would be tough, but I was determined. My meditation had yielded a strong sense of Divine Love with me, and I was sure that if I linked up with that Divine Power, there wasn't anything I couldn't accomplish that day! I must admit, I wasn't truly prepared for the challenge that was to come. What I thought would be a relatively straight forward uprooting, turned into an intricate root system that was not to be bypassed. I knew there was still life there, and boy did the strength of those roots shout that message loud and clear. There was no getting under them as they were so deep and so vast. The only way to release the bush was to yield all the strength I could muster with my shovel to break the bond of those roots.

    My first pause, to get some wind and wipe the sweat off my brow, consisted of an encouraging round of self-affirmations as I acknowledged that with such a Divine Power on my side, I could do anything. I was determined that these roots would not stop me. I forged ahead, making only a little progress on the mighty root system that seemed unfazed by my efforts. In my second break to reassess, I noted that I could, in fact, wait for Jere to get home from work. Of course he could do it. He always knew how to muscle through the most challenging of roots. But this had become a battle of will, and I really needed to show myself that with trust and God I could do anything. I needed to show myself that I could get past my own limiting beliefs about myself if I just didn't give up. I couldn't let myself quit. I wasn't alone, and I knew I had it in me…somehow. I forged ahead with more persistence and determination than I'd ever known on such a project. I was sweating from head to toe and half-covered in dirt by the time something finally popped, showing signs of release. Ahh, hope! I kept on pounding and chiseling and finally was able to set the remains of the dried out rose bush free of its powerful roots. I fell back on the ground in relief and then heard

Lesson One: Our Bond Is Unbreakable

a sympathetic voice whisper, "You thought that was tough. Our bond is unbreakable." That statement has since replayed in my head a thousand times, and I still get teary-eyed every time I think of it.

The experience created for me what in counseling we often call, "a felt sense." In other words, at that very moment, I knew with every fiber of my being how incredibly strong and genuinely unbreakable is the bond that Divine Love shares with me. The Voice was undeniable, and the felt experience of the strength of that root was forever imprinted within me. Whenever I think about the unbreakable bond I share with Love Itself, I remember the mighty roots of that rose bush and know it's a force that cannot be reckoned with.

I believe I was able to hear that powerful message because I had opened my day with meditation and a willingness to listen to what Love Itself wanted me to understand. I had been steadfast in acknowledging I was not alone in that endeavor and that openness to listen allowed me to hear what I otherwise wouldn't. Even now that's a lesson I want to remember. Oh, If I could only get more consistent at staying in direct communication with Divine Love throughout every day. I wonder how many more reassuring messages Love Itself has yet to share with me.

A couple years have passed between this powerful experience and the writing of this book. Jere and I were recently sitting out on our back deck soaking in Love's presence surrounding us. It was Jere, ironically, not me, who first noticed that the bush I planted on that very day is now in full bloom and has grown into the shape of a lovely heart! It took a moment for me to grasp the depth of such a lovely sign of Love's presence blooming in red roses right in front of me!

Love Itself wants you to know that you are no exception. The bond you share with Divine Love is just as reliable. Whether you realize it or not does not affect that truth. There is a rose bush revelation waiting for you to experience. God is always speaking to you. Are you letting your mind be still enough to hear? In every moment we have the choice to listen either to the Voice of Love Itself within us or the voice of our own judging, separated self. The more we let ourselves tune our ears to ask what Love wants us to know, the more we realize we are never alone and come to recognize the strength of an unbreakable bond. Now that I think of it, if I hadn't depended on a force greater than my own all along, I would've simply given up my endeavor to free the rose bush. And consequently, I would have missed out on Divine Love's message altogether.

Lesson One: Our Bond Is Unbreakable

Take 5 to 15 minutes to sit in silent meditation before each *Message of Love*.

Repeating segments of the following may help guide you...

> *Breathe*
> *Just Breathe*
> *Release*
> *Release*
> *Release*
> *Your striving puts up a wall that blocks you*
> *from receiving the peace, the bliss,*
> *the blessings I have for you.*
> *Yes, for you*
> *Breathe*
> *Let Me in*
> *I come to you at each moment.*
> *Feel My breath in you.*
> *Just breathe.*

Next, repeat each *Message of Love* slowly one or two times, allowing yourself to consider that Love Itself is waiting to speak directly to you.

You may choose to then follow the writing prompts to more fully clarify and expand upon the concepts within or create your own.

Let this be *your journey* to remembering the truth of your worth.

Message of Love 1:
A Little More

Every moment, every week, will we together learn to release a little more; release a little more of the struggle, release a little more of the fight, release a little more of the illusion that you are separate and alone. Return to Me a little deeper. In each moment, rest a little deeper into Me. With each week allow a little more of Me, a little more of our joining, a little more peace, a little more trust, a little more surrendering, a little more joy, a little more bliss.

Learn to breathe with Me. Learn to be with Me a little more, a little more, a little more as you return to find your space of truth, and within that space of truth, your indelible worth, and within that worth, a love that never ends in Me.

....

****Dear Love, I release to you now:
(ex: fear, trying, worry about…)**

**And in releasing I'm ready to allow myself
to begin receiving: (ex: peace, bliss)**

***Today I am willing to release a little more
and allow a little more all through my day.**

....

Lesson One: Our Bond Is Unbreakable

Message of Love 2:
Loved Beyond Measure

Are you open to Love?
If it came to greet you, would you notice?
Or would you be absorbed in thought about some hurt from yesterday?
Or stolen away with your face buried in the news?
If Love arrived
Nay, if Love were already by your side,
Would you notice?
Would you allow yourself to receive it?
Or is there some long-lost fear deep within you
That it must not be for you?
For you don't think you are worthy.
Look up, My child,
Love is here beside you
Speaking your name
Softly waiting for you to look up
And know It waits for you.
You are loved beyond measure.
Beyond anything, you have ever allowed yourself to imagine.
Consider the flowers.
Each so uniquely shaped and colored,
with twists and turns and blossoms flowing out in every angle.
You are no less beautiful,
no less unique.
You are cherished beyond measure.
You exist to bloom,

to grow, to extend your colors, your light out, always outward.
For you are Love,
Extending out from Love,
Extending out from the comforting arms of Love Itself.
Released in complete safety
Always safe, always protected
And completely free to extend ever outward
That which you are…
Beauty, Light, Love without limits.

....

**Take a meditative walk in nature. Be open to love. Acknowledge your willingness to receive Love Itself speaking to you by noting, "I'm open to hearing whatever you would have me hear and seeing whatever you would have me see." Note any insights or reflections:

*Today I will look for love wherever I go, whatever I do.

....

Lesson One: Our Bond Is Unbreakable

Message of Love 3:
Wake Up

As a mother bird calls to her children to wake up and be fed, so it is, I too, am calling to My children, wake up and listen! I have life-giving messages to share with you still. Wake up from your complacency in the humdrum life that you are living. Wake up from your fear and self-doubt. Wake up and be fed by My words of love and compassion and hope! My will for you is perfect happiness, perfect completion in Me and joy beyond your wildest dreams. Return to Me, My children.

Be still and listen.
I Am speaking to you still.

....

**I'm willing to begin considering that these Messages of Love are meant specifically for me. I'm willing to recognize that I was led to these Messages for a reason and so I allow myself to consider what it means to me that Divine Love Itself is speaking directly to me and wants me to know:

*Today I breathe in the peace of realizing, Love Itself longs for me to draw close. I will awaken and look for Love's presence throughout my day.

....

Message of Love 4:
Hear My Voice

Do you not realize, I am always here to speak with you? Let yourself sink into the awareness of My deep love for you, perhaps as you revel in the songs of the birds or notice the glimmer of sunlight on a dewy morning. For if you allow yourself, in each moment, to feel the deep love I have for you in every note of nature, then do you raise yourself to the consciousness of Me. Then will you tune your ear to hear My Voice of love calling to My creation. Know who you are. Know whose you are. Live your life in Me. My breath in you is a bliss that we both can share.

**Dear Love, Thank you for your presence in all of nature. Today I see you and hear you in:

*Today I will let myself sink into awareness of the deep love that God has for me. I will be mindful to breathe in this truth with every breath.

Lesson One: Our Bond Is Unbreakable

Message of Love 5:
It is Certain

It is certain
I will come
You cannot look Me in the eyes
For that is a vastness you cannot understand
But each time you close your eyes
You see Me
And I see you
As you melt back into me
And we float together in the vastness of creation
Do not fear
It is certain
Our thoughts will merge
And I will guide you
To the greatest desires of your heart
For they are mine too
Our shared will
will evolve
Just close your eyes
And wait for me
I will come
It is certain
Do that which you need to do
But be excited about that which is unfolding
We have much to do
You and I

So go forth in your day with joy
Knowing I step with you into each moment
Toil, strife, and worry are not for you
Not for the one
Who walks with the will of Creation
Alongside
Go joyfully forward
With a light step
We cannot fail
It is certain.

....

**Reread the Message slowly. Be still and just breathe. Read the Message out loud to yourself. Be still and breathe again. Write whatever comes:

*Today I return in each moment to the peace of knowing and trusting, Love Itself walks with me. It is certain our shared will, will evolve.

....

Lesson One: Our Bond Is Unbreakable

Message of Love 6:
I Am Here

Any child of Mine—and you are all My children—who seeks earnestly to know Me, will find Me within themselves. For I am known by many names, but in truth no name can complete the description of that which I Am. So do not limit yourselves with names or conditions by which to find Me and know your truth in Me. Simply trust I Am here for all, waiting to be known and remembered by all who ask and seek. I Am as near to each as your own breath. I live within you and you in Me. Go within and you will find Me. Look with love on all things, and you will know My presence. No conditions do I give you but that you trust I Am here, waiting for you; each of you.

....

****Today I release all the conditions/
expectations I place upon myself:**

(Ex: The need to please others or do things perfectly.)

**I will remind myself all day that Love
Itself loves me exactly as I am.*

....

Message of Love 7: Enwrapped With Me

I am not just the vine,
I am your vine, coursing through your being.
Can you not feel me in the vibration of your breath?
The steady rhythm of your pulse
tapping its melody in each fiber, each strand of your DNA?
My child, you have forgotten so much of your truth
when you let go of your knowing
of the branch of life
we are together, as One.
You've forgotten the very essence of your Truth,
which is forever enwrapped with me,
Forever My Love extending
Expressing
As my beloved, cherished, treasured child.
Return to me, oh my Beloved One.

**I've never quite considered how intricately woven I am with My Source. I'm seeing now that my deepest passions and joys take their root in Divine Love. My passion and love of the following are part of the very essence of my Truth:

*Today I honor and embrace my Truth within.

Message of Love 8:
With You Always

Do not wait for the perfect conditions to seek My love and presence. For I am with you always. It matters not if there are peace and quiet surrounding you or if you are amid noise or chaos, tears, or upset. Call me and come to Me under any circumstance. I will be there, ready to commune with you and offer you the steadfast support and guidance that you need. There is no condition that would keep Me from you. Remember this and seek Me always. My love, presence, and power are with you forever. The more often you remember this and allow My voice to speak to you, the more you will feel the joy of our connection.

....

**Dear Love, I remember my connection with you first by noticing my breath. As I breathe in and out, I remember you are breathing with me in each inhale and exhale. I rest here with you and allow myself to feel your nearness in words or stillness:

*Today I want to remember:

....

Message of Love 9:
Return to Me

Like waves in the ocean, your awareness of My presence forms then falls to retreat back to sea. Allow yourself to ride these waves without fear of losing the flow of the current. For it will always come in and yet withdraw again, as the forms of the manifested world draw your attention away from the truth of My presence.

Rest, in the knowing, I am always here, and the wave of your awareness will quickly return as you come back to the silence and release the outer world for a while to be with Me. In time you will learn life is more fluid and more joyful when you often return to Me, to ride the wave of My peace within you.

....

**I'm learning that my feelings are strong indicators of how close I am to you. For whenever I am feeling at peace, whole, and loved, I know I am listening to your Voice in me. Whenever I am feeling down or discouraged, I am cutting myself off from Your truth in me. When I am close to you, I feel and remember:

*I will be patient with myself today and notice when I am letting myself draw near or far from You.

....

Lesson One: Our Bond Is Unbreakable

Message of Love 10:
Complete in Me

My net is cast wide to all My children. I see no differences in who one chooses to love or be. I seek only that you each know My love and know who you are at one with Me. I speak to no one in particular and yet I speak to all as one. You are all, united, My children, with no exceptions. Our bond is unbreakable, which is a concept you can scarcely comprehend. No conditions do I place upon you, except that you be you, exactly as I created you. Try not to walk in another's shoes or judge the path they alone have chosen. It is not for another to say who is welcome in My kingdom and who is not. My kingdom, being love, is only love. And that is all it shall remain despite your limited view from a vantage point that is far too small to realize the grandeur that is all. Rest awhile, My child. Rest from your categorizing, analyzing, and second-guessing the nature of My love. For all are complete in Me, where nothing is lacking, ever, but your realization you have never left your Creator, nor the Divinity that is you.

....

**As I accept the truth of these words, I want to start today to let myself more fully be me, exactly as I am. To me, embracing and being myself exactly as I am means:

*I remember today, I am exactly as I was created to be!

....

MEDITATION

There Is an Ancient Song Which Calls to You
It is a melody you remember well
Of who you are and where you're from
It calls to you from the silent spaces of your mind
And beckons you to listen, to remember
The deep love that holds you
Forever in Its Mind
A love which will never leave
And yet never forces any will upon you
Other than your own
A love of perfect freedom
Who sees you only in the light of your true being
And keeps you safe forever from your dreams
Of separation and fears of abandonment
And in the presence of this melody
This ancient song
So peacefully it carries you
Beyond your thoughts of time
To memories of your perfect safety
Perfect Wholeness
And greatest Joy
It calls you Back
To remember who you are and have always been
It is your space of truth
The Unbreakable Bond of Love Itself

LESSON TWO:

I Am Ever Your Guide

There is a symphony keying up for you.
Millions of angels are fine tuning their instruments
In preparation for your willingness to join
them in the grand unfolding of all
God created you to become and expand into.
There is excitement in the air
And anticipation as your energy rises
and they, in unison, feel you
Elevating to their presence.
For it is the space where you can receive and synchronize
with all the harmonies of their instruments.
Joy is palpable at the certainty of your expansion.
The unfolding of all that you are,
And all the Love you have to offer,
~The Love of All That Is~
Gearing up to fully express through you.
Revel in the tingling sensation of knowing
How dynamic a Power is not only supporting,
But carrying you on the wings of eagles,
As our unified Will expands out before you.
Ahh bliss
Ah joy! Ah elation in the unfolding!

Lesson Two: I Am Ever Your Guide

"Your present trust in Him is the defense which promises a future undisturbed, without a trace of sorrow and with joy which constantly increases as this life becomes a holy instant, set in time but heeding only immortality. Let no defenses but your present trust direct the future and this life becomes a meaningful encounter with the truth that only your defenses would conceal."
~**ACIM OrEd WkBk.135.20**

"A Course in Miracles asks you to "receive instead of plan," and yet few of you understand the meaning of this simple instruction or what it says to you of the unknown.
 What it says is that the unknown is benevolent. What it says is that what you cannot anticipate can be anticipated for you. What it says is that you could be receiving constant help if you would but let it come. What it says is that you are not alone."
~**ACOL C:17.7 C:17.8**

It was a Saturday night, and both my 24-year-old son and I had made attempts to call each other, but each time the other was tied up with someone and couldn't talk. A year ago, he moved several states away to Colorado to follow his dream of working on space exploration while also getting to ski during his downtime. By the time I had thought to try him one more time I was a bit tired and didn't have the energy for a conversation. So, I decided to wait and trust that he must be having a full day and we would connect tomorrow instead.

It was getting past my usual 10:00 pm bedtime, and so I got up to begin getting ready for bed.

On my way to brush my teeth, I felt an impulse to just text Brennen to check in despite my earlier decision to wait. *I picked up my cell, and as my finger hovered just over the first number, it rang.* Brennen's name displayed, and I felt immediate confirmation that we were meant to talk. It seems often that he tends to call when he's on my mind anyway. I laughed as I explained to him that my finger was just about to touch the phone to text when he called. He exclaimed, "well, that's telling, given the situation I'm in right now." My son went on to explain that he was driving in the worst road conditions he'd ever been in. Not something a mother ever wants to hear!

He was 5 miles out from a small town on Copper Mountain, Colorado on the way to meet his friends for skiing in the morning. The roads were covered in a thick sheet of ice, and he and the line of cars following him were driving 5 mph on the side of the road going downhill. He explained that he had just done a 360 spin on interstate 70 noting that before the tunnel, the roads weren't too bad and thus, most drivers, like himself, came out of the tunnel driving far too fast for the conditions.

As he talked, he saw another car spin and commented as he watched that driver follow suit and join the caravan behind him on the side of the road. He then laughed a nervous laugh noting, "at least everyone is going so slow now that all accidents are happening in slow motion." He eased my mind noting lots of cars in ditches and plenty of fender benders but, "no one's going to die here tonight. It's like a slow-motion movie." Nonetheless, I could tell he needed a soothing voice on the line to help him continue as he rode his brake down the icy mountain hill. The phone reception cracked in and out and sometimes he cut out altogether.

I reassured him I wasn't going anywhere, even if the phone did go dead. And he knew from previous experience that I would see him through to his destination even to the point of calling the highway patrol if needed. I soothed and bored him for the next 45 minutes with insights about the coming attractions in the town he was approaching as I had found his location on my GPS. At last, he noted that he had arrived to meet his friends and had to get off the phone to figure out where to park and enter. We ended our conversation, but he knew I wouldn't be going to bed until I had confirmation he was clearly safe with his friends. About 10 minutes later, he finally texted me that he had found them all and signed off with, "I love you."

As I lay in bed, I marveled at the impulse to text him to begin with, thinking about how Spirit had surely guided that entire interaction. If I had gone to bed at my usual time, just ten minutes earlier, I probably would not have even heard the phone ring.

The next day I awoke with a realization that the entire experience with Brennen was a perfect metaphor for the Message of Love I had just received and written the previous morning. Just as I had reassured my son that I was not going anywhere, no matter how bad the connection, Love Itself had relayed that very same message that morning. Is this a Message you also are needing to hear?

Come, Come, Come.
Come rest with Me a while.
Rest from the cares and worries That
weigh heavy on your heart.
Come
Rest
Rest here with Me.
Enter My presence as you breathe
In then Out.
Feel Me here.
For I am always here.
Feel the doors of your awareness open unto you.
As you breathe, here with Me.
And remember how I remain here steadfast.
Waiting for you.
Ever, patiently, lovingly, I wait for your return.

> Come, My child, through the doors that open wide for you.
> Come to Me and find your rest from the
> weariness of the world of separation.
> Let the thoughts of fear, of separation
> and isolation fall off you
> like a heavy cloak you no longer need.
> And now, free, here with Me, do you
> enter the Power of our union.
> The altar of creation.
> Your rightful place with Me.
> **~Love Itself**

Love Itself remains here, steadfast, waiting for you, no matter how poor the connection.

Are you receptive? Are you slowing down to listen? Will you allow yourself to open to the power, strength, and guidance that is waiting patiently and lovingly for you, always?

Take 5 to 15 minutes to sit in silent meditation before each *Message of Love*.

Repeating segments of the following may help guide you...

Breathe
Just Breathe
Release
Release
Release

Lesson Two: I Am Ever Your Guide

Message of Love 1:
Relax Into the Ride of Life

I want to continue to speak to you of life, the life which you are learning to accept your worthiness to receive. For you have lost your way and, in some cases, have not yet found your way. Take heart, the path will always, in your time, return you back to Me. The life I have created for you now, in this moment, is so much more than you've allowed yourself to experience. You have taught yourselves and one another to rely far too much on your own doing and therefore have missed the peace that comes with trusting your guide. It is as though you are on a river ride with an expert guide who knows every twist and turn, rock and current, and yet you would take the ore for yourself and insist on doing it your way. You end up with far more stress and struggle and heartache. When all along you could've been sitting peacefully in your seat enjoying, nay savoring, the beauty along the way. I long to be your guide but you must learn to let go and relax into the ride of life. I will not fail you.

....

**As I learn to relax, let go and let Love Itself steer my boat, I savor the gifts of this holy instant. I close my eyes, just breathe, and begin to rest into my body, my chair, and Love supporting me. When I open my eyes, I take 5 minutes to soak my awareness deeply into each color, shape, smell, sound, and sensation that surrounds me:

*In trusting my guide today, I practice being fully present for each holy instant.

....

Message of Love 2: ## My Strength Will Not Fail You

I have told you before, I have come that you will have life. Now, after a long journey back to Me, you are coming to understand and know this life in Me for which I spoke. It is a life where every burden you give to Me, even before you allow it to become weighted with any cares or worries. It is a life of complete surrender to the knowing that I am a perfect guide and the journey I have prepared for you is safe and sure and filled with eddies of unbridled surprises, happy moments, and fragrances so sweet. Perhaps there will be bumps and rocks and currents along the way that may threaten your peace. But you will take heart, for I am an expert guide, and My strength will not fail you. I will never fail you. On Me you can be sure. Rest well, My child. Enjoy this blessed life. It is My love for you.

....

**I want to take some time now to envision my journey with you when I am in complete surrender and trust. I see this journey that is safe, sure, and filled with happy moments will look and feel something like this:

*Today I breathe in ease and peace and joy, as I begin a new journey of blissful trust and surrender.

....

Message of Love 3:
The Flow of My Supply

Do you see how your pet follows you and comes to be always at your side? So too must you learn to walk in constant companionship with Me. The closer you stay to Me, the deeper your peace, the more the flow of My supply stays ever open and moving to and through you. Simply stay near and rest always in Me.

**I admit sometimes I have trouble staying near to you, oh Love. The ego-mind keeps me constantly distracted from your presence. I'd like to begin a practice that calls me back to an awareness of your constant companionship throughout my days. I'm going to contemplate this and commit to my new practice here:

*Thank you, Love for your constant supply that flows ever through me as I walk in union with You.

Message of Love 4:
Give Each Outcome to Me

Guard yourself carefully. Learn to tune and tend to each tightened muscle, each moment when you feel weighed down by tasks and worries you think you must figure out and accomplish alone. At the slightest awareness that you have forgotten I am with you, and on your team, compel yourself to pause and return to Me. Return to our shared breath. Return to our shared mission. Return until all tension eases, and again you feel the ease and joyful anticipation of all I'm working out for you. Give each outcome to Me and look with My joyful gaze upon all of creation unfolding in perfect harmony.

....

**I revel in the remembering that I need do nothing alone today. I breathe easy and my body lets down as I give the outcome of all my concerns and tasks to you this day:

*A note to myself I will carry in my pocket today: "Remember, dear one, you walk with Love Itself by your side. You need do nothing alone today!"

....

Lesson Two: I Am Ever Your Guide

Message of Love 5: Ever Your Guide

I AM a rainbow.
I Am a tree.
I Am a flower, opening and free.
I Am the colors of the sky, melding into one
Majestic, I fly.
Through time and space, I float, I drift, I
soar on high and dive down deep.
I Am you.
You are Me, freely extending all love, encompassing.
A river of power mighty and strong.
A gentle ripple on a soft summer pond.
I swirl through galaxies light years apart.
Glowing, sparkling in stars, radiating My heart.
Everywhere I flow.
I'm love growing, allowing, passionately, liberating, free.
Can you feel?
Can you see?
Do you know with your soul?
The twinkling sparkle of dew on the grass,
Something calling, a lullaby blowing past.
The silence, a quiet pause between the strokes of a clock
Beyond time, out of time
A holy instant of knowingness
In the stillness of night
The release of each breath

A gentle knowing
Spirit Am I
Ever your Guide
To My beloved child of Divine

....

**I want to embrace this truth of my divinity in union with Love Itself. In some ways it's hard to grasp and yet in other ways it feels so obvious. I am a creator, one with all that is. Today (or this week) I will take time to create and celebrate the divine unfolding that is me, in union with Love Itself. Perhaps I will walk, dance, paint, write, sing, cook...whatever is in me that longs to express the love that I Am. I commit to it here:

*I Am one with all that is, expanding only Love. I Am unlimited potential.

....

Lesson Two: I Am Ever Your Guide

Message of Love 6:
Countless Signs of My Love and Care

In any given moment I am bombarding you with support and life sustaining, even life thriving messages, signposts, and opportunities which are opening passages for your greatest joy, peace, and ease. Countless signals of My love and care for you abound and surround you. Yet your defenses of striving and trying, fixing & analyzing create walls of resistance which keep you from noticing and therefore receiving the very answers you seek.

You must come to Me every hour, even every minute to pause and release your defenses and allow My love, My light, My blessings to fall around you. Let Me enfold you with all that you need to thrive in this abundant world I have created for you. Then and only then will you feel the wind lift you and carry you to the bliss of being with Me. Then and only then will you realize the birds' songs are sung for you. And the seeds of the Maple scatter all about you to let you know the endless, abundant supply always there for your every need, nay your every desire. Then and only then will you notice and inhale the sweet fragrance of My Love in every flower and scent of nature created just for you. And see that the birds soar above your head in reminder of the incandescent freedom you are given in union with Me. The sunshine flickering upon the leaves, casting light and shade in perfect accord; all of it and so much more for you when you simply rest in Me. Remember Me. Release all to Me.

....

**Dear Love, this reality you speak of is a blissful truth I want to embrace and accept. I begin by noticing the signs and opportunities you have already placed before me in my life:

....

— 57 —

And I acknowledge the defenses like striving and fixing I need to let go of:

*I am being guided by countless signs and moments of love and care today. I am open and willing to see and receive all of them!

Message of Love 7:
The Way of Pure Light

Living the way of trust in Me is as vital as sleep is to the body. It is as necessary as food to nourish you. Living a life of trust in Me is the way of joy and freedom to the soul. Trust in Me as you rely on air to breathe. Take no step without first allowing Me to show you the way.

And trusting that My way for you is one of perfect peace and your greatest joy. A life of trust in Me is no idle truth. It is breath. It is nourishment. It is the way of pure light. It is the way you were created to live.

....

**When I am letting go of ego messages of fear and striving, I free myself to soak in the nourishment and supply I truly need. As I let go and trust today, I celebrate all that is unfolding beautifully in my life (knowing it is here within me even before my eyes can see it):

*I affirm, "I Am one with all Love who lights my path and leads the way to my perfect peace and greatest joy."

....

Message of Love 8:
A Little More Trust

Try trusting just a little more today. Just take one step with a little more trust, a little more willingness to let Me show you My presence, My power, and My care for you. Just try a little more trust and a little less need to defend or protect the ego-mind. For when you trust a little more, then can we work together as one, as one flowing energy from the Unified Field into the manifested world of form. Just a little more trust is all it takes, and a little less ego, which you no longer need. Oh, just try and you will see all I long to show you. For together, what a symphony are we.

....

**I'm trying a little more trust today by (Name specifically what you will do differently as you let trust lead instead of your ego-mind.):

*As I trust a little more today, I open my eyes to see Love's care and power lining all up for me.

....

Lesson Two: I Am Ever Your Guide

Message of Love 9:
Join the Unified Field of Pure Love

You are simply learning to tune your vibration to Me. This requires your willingness to acknowledge your worthiness to receive Me. To forgive yourself first is a necessary step.

Although, you are never truly in need of forgiveness. You must first allow yourself to be free of your perceived inadequacies and beliefs in your shortcomings. When once you realize and accept your true worthiness to be linked, forever one with the love that is All, then are you ready to tap into our unified field of all that is. Therefore, do you tap into all power, all knowing, all truth. You, My child, are realizing this. You are ready and now able to receive. You are simply learning now to recognize your worthiness to connect and receive our union within each moment. So exciting is the freedom, the vastness, that comes of your readiness to receive.

For now, is nothing out of reach. And there is no miracle that cannot unfold in our unified field of pure love. Bask in this worthiness to receive. Know that you have been called because you are meant to be moving in harmony with all that is.

....

**I'm ready to begin forgiving myself for my perceived shortcomings so that I may be free to accept my worthiness to join the unified field of all love. I'm beginning to forgive myself for:

*I ask Love Itself today to help me release all self-judgment and accept my worthiness to join in our unified field of only love.

....

Message of Love 10:
Unnecessary Pressure

Your physical discomfort is simply a reflection of the pressure you put upon yourself. Your perception that you need to make everything happen, your striving to figure out how to get everything done and how to provide for yourself just puts unnecessary pressure upon yourself. Such pressure blocks your allowing of My power. Return to Me, to your natural state of grace, where you trust in our power and allow Me to show you. In your natural state you know there is nothing you need to do of your own accord. Surrender all to Me and trust that I will show you, carry you, and open every door. All is prepared and ready for you. Release your striving. Surrender all to the bliss of our united power!

....

**I'm going to do something out of character for myself today. When I'm tempted to push and pressure myself, I'm going to let go and trust. I'm going to trust in the power of our union and let go of any efforts to do anything on my own today in regard to accomplishing the following:

*I release all striving today. Instead, I walk in grace as I allow the power of Love Itself to guide and support me in every moment of this day.

....

Meditation

As I Awaken today in Love
May I remember what I Am
For I Am Spirit
May I remember where I Am
For I Am in the mind of God
May I allow myself to Awaken
In this natural state
For in my natural state there is
No effort at all
And so, I arrive in grace
Each moment
Now and in the next
Simply as I Am
Completely Whole, Safe, and Love Itself
May I allow the ego-mind to remain
resting on my bed stand
For I choose to value nothing of myself today
But the love that I Am
May I breathe easy, my body relaxed
And each cell Awaken
To the Joy and Peace of arriving
In grace each moment of this day.
(As Published in Unity Magazine)

LESSON THREE:

Trust Wholly in Me

One small step of trust
Then another
Then an opening appears
Where you thought was a wall
And soon another
And another
Until you discover the room you thought you were standing in
Is an open field of infinite possibilities.

"In the holy instant, the power of the Holy Spirit
will prevail because you joined Him."
~ACIM Or.Ed.Tx.16.76

"No miracle can ever be denied to those who
know that they are one with God."
~ACIM Or.Ed.WkBk.124.6

"You are patient, loving, and kind. You have entered the time of tenderness. You begin to hear what your feelings are saying to you without the interferences and cautions of your thinking mind. You begin to trust and as you begin to trust you begin to extend who you are. True giving and receiving as one begins to take place. You have entered Holy Relationship."
~ACOL Addendum—Learning in the Time of Christ A.14

A short while ago I had another most powerful experience of Love Itself awaking me with a vision accompanied by a loving message. Even after so many messages and conversations with Love Itself I often still find it difficult to get my head around the reality of what I have been experiencing and to accept that this is real. It's remarkable how powerful the denial mechanisms of the ego-mind can be. Yet, I also recognize the fear and uncertainty that so many are experiencing right now. I know in my heart that Love Itself has reached through to me at this special time, with the knowing that I will share with those of you who are open and willing to receive the depth of hope, love, and encouragement revealed within. This message has brought me such certainty and peace, perhaps you will be able to join me in receiving such immense hope and perfect peace. Moreso, perhaps you will be more open to hearing what Love Itself would have you hear as well.

I had been feeling frustrated by my daily meditation as I was clearly trying too hard to feel the power of connection with Love Itself. When my body lets go and my mind unlocks there comes a certain feeling of pure release and then a sense of lifting into what feels like another realm. On this particular morning, it wasn't happening. I knew I was trying too hard and yet the more I tried, of course, the more distant I felt. I let go for the day and trusted in Love's presence despite the clear blocking of my ego messages.

When I went to bed that night, I tried again to let go and was able to drift off to sleep with a greater awareness of God's presence. I awoke a little before my alarm and let myself drift back to sleep in a meditative state. It was soon thereafter that I was awakened to an awareness of that sense of being lifted into another realm. It was the space for which I had tried too hard to experience in my morning meditation. Spirals of light appeared and then something new; a small heart made of sparkling diamonds, floated in a soft, white cloud in front of me. As I basked in the beauty of this dazzling heart, I heard these loving words,

> *"Whatever you ask in My name and in union with Me, wholly trusting in the power of our union, then it shall come to pass."*

The vision then gently dissipated into swirling patterns of the single eye. I laid in awe and wonder reveling in the power of these words and trying to get my head around the whole experience. I realized then the significance of the instruction, "wholly trusting in the power of our union." The wholly trusting part is what can be so difficult. Of course, after such a powerful moment, it was much easier for me to wholly trust! I eagerly lifted some of my most pressing concerns to Love Itself in that moment and was most excited about all that would come to pass.

As I got up to prepare my breakfast, I did so slowly, still absorbing the reality of it all. That day, I shared the experience with my husband, Jere, and my youngest son. I deeply hoped they too might be able to take joy in the power of such a message. However, I realize that as hard as it is for me to break through my own denial, it must be that much harder for others to accept the full reality that the creator of the universe is truly speaking to me. Paradoxically, Jere sometimes laughs at my remarkable disbelief when he is often more convinced than me that this is all real. Perhaps his Catholic upbringing, instilled in him a bit more trust in the mystery of Divine ways. I still wonder if my two adult sons, while immensely supportive, must still wonder if their mother is a bit off her rocker!

With first small and now growing steps of wholly trusting in the power of my union with Love Itself, I'm seeing firsthand, how all does truly come to pass. I've marveled at the unique and unexpected ways these manifestations of my prayers (united will) have unfolded noting the ones that come the quickest arrive when I have no doubt of my worthiness to receive and thus do not hinder it with undue worry or effort.

A few months have passed, and I still find myself going in and out of my own ability to wholly trust, in other words, to accept the full reality of the power of this union. Yesterday, I sat pondering the fear and uncertainty of the COVID-19 virus moving through the

Lesson Three: Trust Wholly in Me

world. I wondered what comforting words Love Itself might have me share. The resounding message I heard from Love was, "that all may know the power of our union." Shortly thereafter I turned to a short study of A Course in Miracles and stopped in awe at the validation of the following text,

> **"In the holy instant, the power of the Holy Spirit will prevail because you joined Him."**
> ~Or.Ed.Tx.16.76 ACIM

When we allow ourselves to recognize that Love Itself/God is right here, right now breathing within us and with us, we enter the holy instant (eternity/full union). From this space we can release the limitations of our small self and join in the co-creative power of all Love. When we are wholly trusting in the power of this union, our bodies relax, our immune system strengthens, we feel hopeful and joyful and thus see opportunities and solutions we would otherwise miss if we were limited by fear and worry.

We allow ourselves to see the miracles before us and the places where Love would guide us to go, and the insights God would have us know. Wholly trusting allows us to receive the gifts of guidance, joy and creative power God wills for us. Know you are worthy now of joining in this union and wholly trusting in its Power.

Can you think of a time when you wholly trusted and surrendered to the power of Love Itself? Has God ever let you down when you did fully trust and surrender to the power of this union? Have you let yourself acknowledge your worthiness to receive the power of such a union?

Take 5 to 15 minutes to sit in silent meditation before each *Message of Love*.

Repeating segments of the following may help guide you...

Breathe
Just Breathe
Trust
Trust
Trust

Lesson Three: Trust Wholly in Me

Message of Love 1:
The Light of My Presence

Attune yourself daily to your natural state of ease with Me. Come first to your breath, then your awareness of the breath I share with you, the life I breathe with you. As you do so, you attune to an awareness of My presence. There will you surrender your worry, your fear, your self-doubt, and striving, all elements of the voice of separation. Shed yourself of these garments and allow the protection of My love to enfold you as a white light illuminates your truth. The light of My presence shines from within you and thus surrounds you and goes with you always.

From this place of peace, trust, and allowing you will see and sense the path I am making clear for you. Follow it without second guessing of the ego-mind. Trust in My power within you. You will see.

....

**As I breathe with Love today, I allow myself to acknowledge Love's presence here within me. I attune to Love's illuminating presence enfolding me and I sense what Love wants me to hear:

*Today I walk with an awareness of Love breathing with me in each moment.

....

Message of Love 2:
Trust in My Vision

See now how I'm lining everything up for you. See the bird high up in the tree. Notice his vantage point far above your own. Trust in My view as well, My ability to see all and know all that you could not possibly see of your own limited vision. Surrender and trust all to Me. Try Me. Try trust in Me, only Me. And watch how all unfolds for you more beautifully than you could ever plan of your own accord.

Know, in My deep love for you, I will make all things new. Simply surrender to our union and trust in My deep love and care for you. You are truly worthy of such deep love. Trust in this. I will not fail you.

....

**I admit there are times when I thought I knew what was best for me and it turned out I was wrong. I needed to accept that Love could see what I couldn't see. I can accept also that my vision may be limited in regard to the following concerns:

*I walk easy today knowing that Love has a much greater view of my needs and circumstances than my own limited vision.

....

Lesson Three: Trust Wholly in Me

Message of Love 3:
Seek My Interventions

It is time now to go forward with joyful anticipation as you seek vigilantly for My intervention and My angel's opening doors, lighting your way, and bringing all into alignment with your new creations. Go forward with expectant knowing that your way is sure. All is well. I walk with you in every moment, nay even more so, there is no moment in which I am not. I am with you in each holy instant, ever more now and now and now. Relish in this knowing.

....

**I'm seeing Love has been guiding me and opening doors in the following ways:

*I expect and look for miracles today.

....

Message of Love 4:
Expanding Love

When dark or dreary days come, tune your attention to all that is pure, lovely, and true.

Focus on the simple joys and remember all for which you feel thankful. As you do so, you will see your reasons to be thankful multiply. For what you put your heart upon will truly grow in expansion as love always does.

....

**Although I may feel worried or down with certain circumstances in my life, I know that Love is still here for me wanting me to know how deeply I am loved. Therefore, I want to let myself receive that love by noticing the many gifts for which I am thankful:

*My heart feels full and expansive as I accept and acknowledge that God is still here, loving me and offering comfort in countless ways, despite my dislike of present circumstances.

....

Lesson Three: Trust Wholly in Me

Message of Love 5:
Trust and You Will Know

There is no order of difficulty in miracles simply because there is no difference in illusions. Illusions are created of an ego-mind, separated from Me, its Source, and perceiving only in judgment and guilt. As you join your mind back into the power of our union, do illusions dissipate and you reclaim your creative power with Me. Thus, miracles are simply extensions of your natural state with Me. They require no effort at all; simply trusting and knowing that I am the true source of all creation. As you trust, you shall know. As you know, you shall experience. As you experience, you shall live in full completion and creative extension with Me.

....

**I want to try to trust a little more today. To trust, however, requires that I accept my worthiness to receive the gifts that come of the power of my union with Love Itself. Today I name one desire that I ask Love to help me first know that I am worthy to receive. As I practice trust in the power of our union, I affirm to myself (with God's help) I am worthy of this miracle:

And I revel in the feelings of having it come to pass:

*I am worthy of miracles because they arrive from my natural state in union with Love Itself.

....

Message of Love 6: No More the Struggle

Trust means letting go of fear. Trust means letting go of control. Trust means choosing first to surrender the fear and the control that you thought kept you safe. Perhaps it did for a while. Choose now a power far greater than your own to carry you beyond all conceptions of your limited form. Trust in Me, My child. Trust in Me. Trust in your union with Me, wherein lies all power you abandoned to experience a life apart from Me. No more the struggle. All I have I give to you. Just release your grasp of the struggle. I've got this now. You can rest now. The dream is over.

....

**I want to remember I don't need to struggle anymore. Like a child coming to its parent with a toy to fix, I bring the following to Love, with complete trust that all will be worked out even more wonderfully than I could ever imagine:

*I choose a life of peace and ease as I choose to live in union with Love Itself.

....

Lesson Three: Trust Wholly in Me

Message of Love 7:
The Mysteries Yet to Be Received

Are you not yet in awe of the miracle of nature playing out before you? Do you not marvel at the intricacies of life that grow and move even beyond your seeing eye? Consider how much more of the intricacies of your own life I am fully ready to orchestrate with your mere willingness to allow yourself to receive. Look more closely, My child, beyond your limited vision. Realize the mysteries of life yet to be received.

....

**The intricacies of nature are truly stunning, amazing, and wonderous. As I tune into the ways Love Itself is orchestrating all of nature, I notice with awe:

*I revel today in the marvelous ways Love Itself can and will orchestrate my life when I open myself to trust and receive. (Write a vision of what that might look like in detail and plant it in a special place.)

....

Message of Love 8:
One Expansion

The reality you think you create is still just that, a creation of your own choosing. Live in the peace and freedom of knowing you call into your own experience only that which you choose. And yet, remember this, in truth, all perception is still illusion. As you join with Me, as you remember your one true self with Me, then will even perception be no more needed, as you return to the knowing of all creation and the One Self that you are within all of creation.

For creation is nothing but your own expansion into all you choose to allow yourself to become and to experience. And thus, as you see it, believe it, and trust in your own expansive unfolding of your one true self, then is it so. It must be. It is certain. For our One expansion cannot fail.

....

**As I contemplate the reality that I am One Self expanding within all of creation I feel: And in this knowing, I choose:

*I am one Love expanding and creating from Divine Power.

....

Message of Love 9:
Wonderous Gifts Around Every Corner

Say to yourself, "My creator in heaven loves and cares for me this much, that Love would give me all the desires of My heart, just as My creator cares for all children of creation. Therefore, I look with joyful anticipation in each moment for the next gift that will be bestowed." When you do so, when you look with joyful anticipation, no forcing, just eager allowing and surrendering, there will you find wondrous gifts, limitless gifts around every corner.

So too must you trust in My love and care for you. Do not resist, even slightly, the encouragement and support I am sending you. Say a whole and hearty thank you and gladly acknowledge your worthiness to receive all support, all encouragement. Thus, do you open the valve free and wide to let more good gifts flow to you!

....

**If I'm honest with myself, I admit that I often resist the encouragement and support Love is trying to offer me. If I look deeper, I acknowledge that it has shown up in the following ways:

*Today I memorize and repeat, "My creator in heaven loves and cares for me this much, that Love would give me all the desires of my heart, just as My creator cares for all children of creation. Therefore, I look with joyful anticipation in each moment for the next gift that will be bestowed." And when I see it, I say, "THANK YOU!"

....

Message of Love 10:
I Will Not Fail You in Your Trust of Me

Do you know how backward you have perceived the laws of My universe to be? It is strange how difficult you have made of something I created to be a dance of perfect ease and perfect trust in the unfolding. And now, you struggle to let go of all that your fearful mind of separation has taught you. In the clinging, do you still deny yourself the perfect flow, a clear open valve for all your inheritance to move uninhibited, freely, easily, and unencumbered.

Simply try, My child. Have a small willingness to simply trust in My words of love to you. *I will not fail you in your trust of Me.* Never will your trust in Me fail to yield the great happiness that is My will for you, nor the abundant life you crave, nor the desires of your heart. Truly I say to you, all creation is ours when you join in trust with the divine power that is ours.

....

**When I think of an Eagle soaring through the sky or a small bird first learning to fly, I contemplate the letting go and trust that comes before the blissful gliding and soaring. If I also choose to let go and live my life like an Eagle soaring, I imagine this is what it would look and feel like:

*Today I pick one small act of letting go as I leap from my own nest and begin to let myself fly.

....

Lesson Three: Trust Wholly in Me

MEDITATION

The Dance of Trust
In the dance of trust
You let Me lead.
You don't have to know the way
But you trust with joy and assurance
That I do.
In the dance of trust
You know there is nothing you
Need to do of your own accord.
And so, you wait upon Me with peace and serenity,
Allowing Me to open the doors
And prompt you gently with spirit impulses
That feel like simple, whimsical steps on a lighted path.
In the dance of trust
You let go all your striving, your trying
To make something happen.
And instead, you allow yourself
To feel the current beneath you
Guiding you, carrying you, and occasionally
Prompting you to put your paddle in the water
Just enough to right and steady yourself
As you easily navigate
The lighted path of glistening water lines
Before you.
In the dance of trust, you take joy in the witnessing,
The revealing of all your desires
Unfolding effortlessly before you
As you surrender to the sweet harmony that is life
In co-creation.

LESSON FOUR:

My Will for You Is Happiness

Do You Know you are worthy of such an extravagant love as Mine?
Dare you to accept such an extravagant love
A love in which you may release all striving
A love in which all peace prevails
And you accept that My will for you is perfect happiness
More so, dare you accept such happiness?
Dare you to accept My offer to dance with you
To guide you, to carry you in My steadfast arms?
Will you choose again
This life with Me
This dance with Me?
Will you choose again to join with Me?
Here in My loving embrace
A child of My own
Inheriting the abundance
Of My kingdom
All here for you
To simply dare to accept
Such an extravagant love
As Mine.
~Love Itself

Lesson Four: My Will for You Is Happiness

"You dwell not here, but in eternity. You travel but in dreams while safe at home. Give thanks to every part of you that you have taught how to remember you."

~A Course in Miracles TX:12.76

"A tiny glimmering of memory has returned to you and will not leave you to the chaos you seem to prefer. It will keep calling you to acknowledge it and let it grow. It will tug at your heart in the most gentle of ways. Its whisper will be heard within your thoughts. Its melody will play within your mind. "Come back, come back," it will say to you. "Come home, come home," it will sing. You will know there is a place within yourself where you are missed and longed for and safe and loved. A little peace has been made room for in the house of your insanity."

~A Course of Love C:10.32

A few days ago, our sweet puppy, Mazzie, stealthily slipped out our back gate while my husband, Jere, was absorbed in his music and transporting brush from our yard. Mazzie loves to chase bunnies! It's evident she was born for this! It is her greatest passion and gives her boundless energy. She's usually happy to by-pass a morning walk and needs a fair share of encouragement to try an afternoon walk. But, oh if there's an opportunity to chase a bunny, suddenly she moves as though she's just had 3 energy drinks.

Now, normally, on such an occasion as this, Jere and I would spend the next 2 1/2 hours chasing her around a 2-mile radius of our house. It's become quite a game to her, and she LOVES it! She darts in and out of the neighbor's bushes happily hiding from us and then magically appearing again if we've lost track of her. We usually end up thoroughly exhausted and recognize all the while that she will only let us catch her when she is good and tired and ready to come home.

This time was different, however. We finally got smart and put a GPS tracker on her. Sure, we chased her for about 45 mins. But then we thought, hmmm, perhaps we should just let her have some fun and we'll sit back and just keep an eye on her whereabouts through our phones. You see, the tracker updates her location at our request, and we can see exactly where she is (at least momentarily) by looking at the app on our phone.

So, we decided to let Mazzie have her fun this time. And we sat, although a bit nervously, down to eat dinner. We had a pretty strong feeling that she knew where home was, and we wanted to see if she would return on her own when she was tired and ready for food and water. Now, Mazzie is a Beagle. Beagles are naturally runners and hunters, and it's not typically in their nature to just come when called as in many of those more-eager-to-please breeds. Hence, most of our research simply suggests at least 5-foot-high fencing to prevent these escapades. Basically, our little experiment felt a tad bit risky.

We tried to enjoy our dinner, but I confess, we were both a little uneasy about this test. It was evening and we had a small window before darkness came and trying to find her small black frame, possibly in the woods and creek behind our home, would be almost impossible.

We sat and ate, periodically checking the GPS to find reassurance that she was still nearby. About an hour and half after her romp began, Jere walked outside to see if she was in site and looking tired yet. Relief flooded through me as I watched him walk in with a very thirsty pup, exclaiming, "look who decided to come home!" He noted that at his first call to her, she came happily running to greet him. Whew!! Our experiment yielded our greatest hope! She did know HOME, and she would eventually decide to return!

Lesson Four: My Will for You Is Happiness

I can only imagine that Mazzie enjoyed following her bliss even more, because she knew what we didn't know she knew. She knew where home was. And.... she stayed close so she couldn't get lost.

Do you ever wonder, if we stayed a little closer to home in our hearts, would that help us to savor and enjoy this life experience even more? Would we be able to embrace the happiness that Love wills for us? After all, Home, Love Itself, is always there tracking us and happily waiting for our return. Can we, like Mazzie, give ourselves permission to run free and play heartily knowing that when we are tired and need to replenish from this adventure, we call life, Love Itself is always waiting and celebrating our return?

....

Take 5 to 15 minutes to sit in silent meditation before each *Message of Love*.

Repeating segments of the following may help guide you...

....

Breathe
Just Breathe
Release
Release
Release

Message of Love 1: Join the Happy Dance

Release, My child, release. Join the happy dance, the union of our souls and our minds.

Together we flow throughout creation. Let go, My child, let go the working, the pressure, the belief you are alone and must make all happen alone. I assure you; an army of angels stands in wait just for you. Take your place with Me, and allow the doors to open before you. Join Me, My child, in the joy of creation, the joy of being the light that we are, united as one love, one light, One without end.

....

**I want to allow myself to envision the army of angels who are always by my side. As I allow myself to feel and accept their presence, I see: (Name colors, sounds, feelings, smells. Describe them in as much detail as possible.)

*Today I acknowledge the loving ones that are always by my side. I'm grateful I get to join in this dance with such love surrounding me.

....

Lesson Four: My Will for You Is Happiness

Message of Love 2:
Know Your Completion in Me

My will for you is happiness. My will for you is peace. My will is that you may know your completion in Me. How can you know this, My child, if a piece of you remains devoted to the struggle, the stress, the worry, and fear? Release your devotion to an illusion that serves you not and perpetuates a lie that hides you, in each moment, from your truth.

Choose joy, My child. Choose freedom. Choose to accept the reality of our union and our co-creative power. Choose again, My child, choose again to ride on the current of My love for you.

There is so much more I would reveal to you. Simply choose joy. Choose love. Choose Me and the power of our union.

....

Dear Love, I want to remember my completion in you. I know it is still deep within my memory. As I search my memory, I recall that being complete in you feels:

And to me it means:

*Today I breathe with You, Love, and remember I am complete in You.

....

Message 3:
Accept My Deep Love

You are wise to remember that your projection makes your perception. For what you see within and hear within, be it My voice or the voice of your separated ego-mind, there will you so perceive and even create the conditions around you. If you recognize and accept My deep love for you and the worthy being that you are, then will you see that love extending out around you.

If you feel small and limited, unloved, and unworthy then will you perceive and create more of that feeling of lack and limitation.

Trust always in My love for you. Always know your worthiness to receive all the happiness and abundance I will for you. Then will that rise to your awareness to be seen and received by you.

....

**Dear Love, when I'm listening to the judging voice of my ego (in my present situation), I hear, feel and perceive:

When I'm listening to your loving voice, I hear:

And I feel, and perceive:

*I commit today to listen to your loving voice instead of the voice of separation.

....

Lesson Four: My Will for You Is Happiness

Message of Love 4:
Divine Unfolding

Embrace joy. Release your need to create struggle by looking for something that is wrong or in need of your fixing. Give yourself permission to receive the happiness that is My will for you. For there is truly nothing wrong and nothing for you to fix. Remember, dear child,

I have given each one the freedom to choose their own path, by which to grow and learn.

And I love each one enough to let them go and decide alone when they choose to return to the care of My presence, which is always there waiting patiently.

Trust in the divine unfolding of My love. All is well. All is well. You are worthy now of happiness. As is each one. Allow yourself to claim your peace with Me. For I celebrate your return as all will one day choose again with Me.

....

**Dear Love, I confess I often create struggle by:

*Today I release the need to struggle and choose again to live in the care of your loving presence.

....

Message 5:
You Are Worthy of Happiness

You must stop your dependence upon external circumstances to allow or disallow your peace and happiness. You are worthy of happiness in every moment, and yet you willingly choose unhappiness and depression, simply because you have not fully claimed your right to be happy in all circumstances. You are worthy of happiness. No one, no other, can claim this for you.

Choose happiness. Claim your right and your inheritance and celebrate that all things are as you wish. For I can only offer all to you. You must do your part and be willing to receive, to accept, the gifts of my Kingdom.

....

**I recognize that self-judgement keeps me from accepting the gift of happiness. I block happiness when I judge myself for:

*Love Itself is not judging me today and so neither will I. I walk in grace today.

....

Message 6:
All Supply is Here

100,000 times, YES! It is true. This is real. Ask and it will be given. Knock and the door is opened. Believe and you will receive. All supply is here ready for the gifting. Celebrate, My child, the keys to the Kingdom are given to you. All is well. All is divine. All is complete. Now and always.

....

**As I trust and believe, so I allow myself to receive the following:

*Today I allow myself to savor the feeling of knowing, the life I choose is already here for me.

....

Message 7: Truly Believe

You have trained yourself to live a life of struggle and yes, often even depression. For within you lies a doubt that you are worthy of happiness and joy, now and always, not just fleeting moments. Perhaps part of this may be some guilt that life should be hard, or you have not done your part. This too must you surrender and trust to Me. Happiness is My will for you, nothing less. Can you allow yourself to live in My will of happiness for you? For if you truly believed in My care and My constant presence always guiding and working everything out for you, then would there be no cause for less than happiness. Do you know you are worthy of all My love and care for you? Do you know, will you accept the gift of happiness that is My will for you? Let go your resistance to joy. And feel My will flow through you. Let happiness come. Welcome happiness as you would welcome Me.

....

**Dear Love, I struggle to fully accept and believe in your care and constant presence because:

I think I need to forgive myself for:

*Today I will try to surrender my resistance to letting Love work things out for my greatest happiness.

....

Lesson Four: My Will for You Is Happiness

Message of Love 8:
Savor My Simple Gifts

Take joy in the simple pleasures of life along your path. Keep ever present to the amusement and play of children and animals. For they are spirits unbound by restraints of the mind. They live more easily in the way of My kingdom and therefore have much to teach you. Revel in their persistence and eagerness to fully absorb the sweet juice of each moment. You have much to remember of life in Me by simply observing and sharing in the pleasure of life with one of these, My young children. For such focus and savoring of My simple gifts will yield your ability to receive an ever-flowing supply from My abundant storehouse.

....

> **Dear Love, thank you for loving me with these simple pleasures in my life:
>
> *Today I choose to notice and savor the simple gifts of your love for me.

....

Message of Love 9:
Choose Only Your Seashells

You, as humans, are easily apt to get caught up in the current of another's emotions. You pick them up as if you are gathering seashells but with little to no thought as to the weight or burden of lifting far more than you have space to carry. Yet, unlike the seashells, you are not even careful in your choosing. You simply notice another would like to give you the responsibility for their feelings and you accept, most often without question. My dear child, I have given to each of My children one's own internal guide of feelings for each alone to explore and choose what lesson they will learn from these. Yet this is not to lay upon another and expect someone outside should fix or ease. Take heart and know you need only choose and explore the seashells of your own feelings.

Leave others, even your closest loved ones, to sort and sift and discover the lessons within their own feelings, as they too take their journey along the beach of life. Allow them the freedom to cast or cherish their own shells as to their own desire.

....

**Dear Love, carrying the weight of another's emotions is one way I rob myself of the happiness you will for me. I can see that I do this when:

*Today I allow myself to choose to accept happiness even when those I love may be struggling to accept their own.

....

Lesson Four: My Will for You Is Happiness

Message of Love 10:
Release Your Loved Ones into My Care

When you accept that you are worthy of happiness, then will you allow yourself to receive the gifts of happiness. This is true for you and for those you love. For when you love others enough to let them choose their own path to accepting their worthiness, then do you fully acknowledge your own worthiness for happiness. For you will no longer allow another's choice for joy or sorrow to determine your own right to claim and receive the happiness which is My will for you. Release your loved ones into my care and, in so doing, give them the freedom to choose and discover their own worthiness as they wish. For the discovery and return to Me will be even more joyful when it is of their own choosing, not yours.

....

**Dear Love, I envision the following people encircled by your loving light:

*Today I lift those I love to Love Itself, trusting that I am worthy of happiness even though they may be struggling.

....

MEDITATION: A HAPPY DAY

I choose to have a happy day today!
I choose to have no judgments and no expectations
Of myself today.
I choose to allow myself to just be me today.
I acknowledge I don't need to please anyone today,
Or be something other than I am
For anyone today.
Today I choose to be free.
To find the simple pleasures in the small
Moments of this day.
Seeking just that…
The simple pleasures and sweet relief
Of not having to fix anything,
Or do anything to earn my worth.
Today I get to be me
~ Simply me ~ All of me ~
~ Lovely me ~
And that gives me a Happy Day!

LESSON FIVE:

The Power of Surrender

I pleaded,
"Help me dear Love to let go of the outcome in this dream."
Love responded,
"It's not about the outcome.
All has already come to pass.
It's about your remembering.
Nothing else."

Lesson Five: The Power of Surrender

"If I live in you, you are awake. Yet you must see the works I do through you, or you will not perceive that I have done them unto you. Do not set limits on what you believe I can do through you, or you will not accept what I can do for you."
~**ACIM OrEd.Tx.10.67**

"There are no battles needed, no victories hard won through might and struggle. This is what is meant by surrender. We achieve victory now through surrender, an active and total acceptance of what is given."
~**ACOL The Forty Days and Forty Nights D:3.7**

It had started out to be a calm evening. I was relaxing in my living room with Mazzie happily perched upon my legs. I had just gotten off the phone with my son and my parting comment was a simple reflection that Lillie seemed to have her haunches up about something. It never occurred to me that the next 30 minutes would soon be turned upside down. In peering over at Lillie, I quickly recognized that she had something small, round, and black that she evidently brought in from the outside, secretly hidden within her mouth. Further scrutiny revealed the unfortunate remains of a mouse which she began to fiercely defend once Mazzie and I noticed its presence.

I got up quickly as I realized a fight could likely ensue if Mazzie would decide to advance closer toward Lillie. Hastily, I suggested heading out for Lillie's favorite activity, a walk. I got up to get the leashes and thankfully had one on Mazzie, just before the war ensued.

Unfortunately, just one leash on Mazzie did little to prevent the two from engaging in a full-on battle. I tried desperately to harness Mazzie into my office and shut the door only to have her lunging out with each attempt, teeth bared and locking onto any piece of Lillie she could find.

Two attempts at separation only yielded my own leg wound from Lillie who thought she was getting at Mazzie and a sore ear which I later discovered was the result of my trying to get the door shut while futilely fighting both dogs off from one another's grasp.

My final and desperate effort to keep them from doing lasting damage to one another found me kneeling on the ground in my office, holding tightly to both dogs' collars and bracing them apart with all my might. I had no idea what would result from this, other than a momentary break, as I peered down at the bright red blood spouting from someplace on Mazzie and checkering the cream-colored carpet. I was out of options and powerless to end this battle. Clearly, it would not end well without some higher intervention. My final attempt came out in breaths of sheer surrender, "Help me, God. Help me, God. Help me, God."

I'm not sure if it was only a minute or five, however, soon after my surrendering words began, Lillie surprisingly let down her guard, stepped backward, walked around the backside of me, and exited the room. As she peered back as if to question her decision, I quickly closed the door behind her, with Mazzie safe inside. I knelt over my desk as I let my shaking muscles recover and breathed silent words of gratitude.

Perhaps a dog trainer could tell me exactly what the secret remedy was that caused Lillie to stop the fight. From a counseling perspective, I can see that I was able to bring pause enough for the triggered fight response of the limbic system to simply release. Yet, as I look back, it took my complete surrender to do so. If I had kept on with engaging efforts to fix things, I would've kept the fight response activated. What we all needed were some long deep breaths and to surrender long enough to let a higher power take over. As I reflected upon it all the next day, I was reminded of the necessity of surrendering to allow the higher power of Love Itself to work through us and for us.

Lesson Five: The Power of Surrender

For me, that surrendering means letting go of the expectations, the fixing, the analyzing, the worrying...basically any thought that comes from the ego-mind. Surrendering these ego antics also means that my worth is no longer attached to any outcome. I was reminded of a conversation I shared with Love Itself only days before. I'm wondering if there is something you also need to surrender to the power of Love Itself. Perhaps this conversation will lend some help:

Love Itself:
Let your mind return into the heart, the One Mind you share with Me. Let no thoughts arise from the thinking mind. For the thoughts you share with Me come only from within the deepest love of our union. Any thought born not of love, of our union, is an illusion, a misperception of the ego-mind. All true thoughts arise from the love of our One Mind hidden deeply within the seed of the heart.

Therefore, I tell you, breathe in My love for you. For it is your allowance of My love that restores your awareness and connection of our One Mind. Breathe in only love. And restore your receptivity to our One Mind.

This takes practice. You have tuned yourself to the voice of the separated mind.

You are learning now to hear and think within your heart chamber. This may feel strange at first, like trying on new glasses. Remember always to let the thinking mind be still. Tune to the love within and have a small willingness to let our One Mind be your guide.

Janine:
It seems you are asking me to stop thinking altogether.

Love Itself:
I am asking you to stop letting the small self (ego) direct you.

Janine:

This is an incredibly freeing concept. And yes, it seems like trying to write with my left hand or putting on new glasses.

Love Itself:
You are better at it already than you think. Even now, at this moment, are you letting My love direct you?

Janine:
Yes, I see. And often I do this when I'm counseling. It feels easier to surrender and let you lead when I have no distractions and outside world expectations.

Love Itself:
Even as you write, your One Mind recognizes that all your expectations are makings of the ego-mind.

Janine:
So, every expectation that I have is a making of the ego-mind?

Love Itself:
Exactly. In the eternal now, there are no expectations. There is simply being the love that you are. There is only pure love. Nothing more is needed. And it is the same on the physical plane. If you could trust in the pure love that you are, then would you see you need nothing. You would see that you are everything, and you have everything. There is nothing lacking within you.

Janine:
Is it even possible to live in this physical body without expectations?

Love Itself:

Lesson Five: The Power of Surrender

Yes, it is a tall order. You see, then, how valuable it is to give yourself time away from daily expectations, so you can strengthen your receptivity to our One Mind, My voice within you.

* * *

This conversation created a new healing method for me. Whenever I notice that my mind is creating inner turmoil, or I'm not feeling the peace of my one alignment with Love Itself, I stop and put my hand on my heart. I breathe slowly into my heart space, and I repeat; "One Mind, One Heart, One Love." This helps me to surrender the meaningless thoughts and expectations and return to my truth, the pure love I share with Love Itself in each eternal and holy instant.

Take 5 to 15 minutes to sit in silent meditation before each *Message of Love*.

Repeating segments of the following may help guide you...

Breathe
Just Breathe
Surrender
Surrender
Surrender

Message of Love 1:
Release the Denial

You are my child. You are not the child of your ego-mind. Release your need to answer to an illusion of separation. It is not real. Your union with Me is all that is real. No longer do you need to defend yourself or prove yourself worthy to a symbol, nay, a creator, of a separated self.

It is not real. I am more real than anything this ego-mind can create. Release the denial of your truth. We are one. There is no ego-mind to answer to. Return to me. Return to the peace of our union. Return to My love, My power, My protection. Surrender your protection of the ego-mind. It knows you not. Your worth, your truth in Me, is indelible.

....

**Dear Love, thank you for giving me a chance to try a life apart from you. And thank you for waiting patiently for me to remember you are still here. Please help me to accept the reality that you are real, and I am one with you. Accepting this truth for me would mean:

*Please help me to hear what you would have me hear and know what you would have me know this day. I am listening.

....

Lesson Five: The Power of Surrender

Message of Love 2: Complete Surrender

If you would know Me and My presence more, if you would free yourself from the world's grip, then you must release your trying and surrender all to Me. You cannot reach Me by your striving. Only in complete surrender do you free your spirit, mind, and body to rise above your focus on earthly form. For in surrendering all, do you allow your energy to be set free and rise unto my chamber. There do you remember you are home, complete in Me. Surrender, My child.

Give up the self-judgment, the shadows of the world's laws, and all beliefs that you have formed that have enabled this dream of separation. Surrender the doubt, the fear, the need for control that supports your fear. Release all to Me and awaken back into My love, where all bliss, all joy, all power waits for you.

....

**Dear Love, I hear you. Today I surrender all of this to you:

*As I release the outcome of all my concerns to you, I rest easy and blissfully trusting in your abundant love and care for me. Thank you for working things out far better than I could do on my own.

....

Message of Love 3:
Just Ask and Allow

I want to speak with you about breaking free of the barriers that block you from realizing the fullness of your truth. While these barriers are merely illusions brought forth from your ego-mind, they feel very real to you. As you allow yourself to acknowledge or accept them, you see they hold great power over you. To that extent, they keep you from realizing how truly limitless you are. Know there is no barrier, if brought to Me, that cannot be completely removed. It is only your doubt that this can be so that keeps you from allowing this release. This is true of all sickness, depression, addiction, control, and even all financial needs. There is not one request or burden, if brought in complete surrender to Me, that cannot be lifted.

Deep within, you know this to be true. For you have found moments where you felt you had no choice but to surrender and so it was, I came to your assistance and your request was met, sometimes tenfold. So funny then, that you can see and experience this truth to be very real, and yet you have not allowed yourself to fully realize it in every area of your life.

Does a flower doubt or struggle to grow from a small seed to a full opening and bloom in all its glory? As Jesus said so many years ago, "Was King Solomon, in all his glory, more arrayed than this?" Why do you worry about all these things when you only have to ask and allow? See how the flower blooms and unfolds effortlessly in its entrustment of all to Me. So too will you unfold as beautifully as the flower, and all your needs will be met when you trust and give all your requests to me.

Lesson Five: The Power of Surrender

....

**Dear Love, here are the barriers I want to surrender into your loving light:

Perhaps I've unconsciously created these barriers as a protection from:

*Today I accept the fullness of my truth in you and gladly give all my self-doubt and barriers to you in exchange for the joyful life you want for me.

....

Message of Love 4:
Meet Me in the Opening

Your mind is a cage that keeps you trapped. Incessantly you cycle through the same thinking patterns over and over, evermore entrapped in an illusion of control and cornered off from any connection to Me, your one true power. To release yourself of the need to think your way into control is the only path to true freedom and joy that comes from living in My spirit.

Your analyzing, regurgitating, reviewing over and over is a trap, a cage within which you will never think your way out.

You must be still. Breathe. Let the ripples of the mind settle. Ride the waves of your breath. There will you find My presence waiting to greet you. Meet Me in the opening where you release thought and sink into the pleasure of being, basking, knowing. It is here your life force awaits. It is here, with Me, all your answers will come. It is here in our connection that all your desires will unfold.

....

**Dear Love, today I surrender my thinking mind to you for at least a little while. I focus on my breathing, and I wait in the opening for you to meet me. It is from within this opening space, I feel/know/experience:

*Today I pause my thinking mind whenever I notice it. Instead, I breathe with you and know you are there.

....

Lesson Five: The Power of Surrender

Message of Love 5:
A Little Willingness

Your ceaseless efforts to think your way into solutions will forever keep you trapped in the illusion of your mind. Just a little willingness is all I ask, a small moment of surrender.

Another small step of trust and one more step, will you then find you are still supported.

More so, you will begin to notice a weightless drifting. Not just in the hard times of life.

You are so mistaken to believe it is only in the hard times that it is okay to surrender. Meet Me in the opening in every moment of each hour. For I am always here, ready to drift with you, to join our flight together through the bliss that life can be, when you let go the entrapment of your mind.

....

**I take some time to draw a cage that represents my mind. I leave the door to the cage open so Love can meet me as I release my need to think and fix things. Within the cage I now name things I can do to bring my awareness to Love's presence within me:

(Ex: savor a cup of tea, focus on the breath I share with Love Itself…)

*I feel peace as I envision my thoughts released to Love and invite God's power to take care of all my needs. I no longer need to fix things on my own.

....

Message of Love 6:
Trust in My Love

You are coming to understand the immense power of surrender. And yet too, you must realize how closely trust must align with surrender. For to surrender all into the power of my loving care, you must first trust completely in My love and care for you and in your worthiness to receive all the blessings and gifts I long to give you. Surrender is a complete and total release of all resistance which many of you may find easier to do perhaps when there are not long held beliefs or expectations about something you should do.

To allow yourself to receive the inheritance I have for you, you must not only surrender the easy moments, but also you must learn to give me every step, every moment of each day, the big and small affairs of your life and heart. And this becomes your work, to trust that I will not fail you. Trust that My love is deep enough and My power great enough that when you let go ~really let go~ of the things, beliefs, and patterns that you have reserved primarily for yourself to manage, when you surrender ALL to me, then you allow the floodgates to open and the deepest desires of your heart to cascade upon you like a brilliant waterfall of glistening diamonds.

This is what I meant when I said you must release everything and follow Me. You must step with enough trust and faith in Me to surrender everything and let Me lead. Let Me give you the greatest desires of your heart. You know what you must surrender. And in the instant that you do so, you will feel the immediate response of My arms and power upon you. I love you this much. And I will never fail you.

Lesson Five: The Power of Surrender

**Dear Love, I'm realizing that I resist your love and care with old patterns, habits, and beliefs. I want to surrender these to you now:

*Today I release resistance to God's deep love and care for me.

Message of Love 7:
Trust in Me

My child, how I long to have you surrender all to Me. Let Me carry you and care for you, as you rest at ease within the safety of My arms. I have orchestrated all to provide for you in boundless ways. You only need to take your place in this grand symphony of Mine. Trust in Me, your conductor, to guide the whole of creation so that our beautiful music will carry throughout time. Trust in this symphony designed in perfection and know you must only bring your gifts, your trust, and your willingness to be led, nothing else. All supply is here in abundance for you. Just allow and let your music sound for all of creation.

....

**Dear Love, thank you for always taking care of me, often beyond my greatest hopes. As I rest with ease within your safe embrace, I envision myself joining you in the symphony. It looks and feels something like this:

*I join the symphony of creation today as I trust, surrender, and let you lead me in this dance!

....

Lesson Five: The Power of Surrender

Message of Love 8:
You Are Not Alone

Anytime you feel heavy or pressured it is because you have forgotten who you are and your natural state with Me. For in surrender of the ego-mind do you learn a life of perfect ease. No more is there need for worry or striving. In allowing yourself to join with Me, you remember the dance of our union and you remember that your part is simply to let Me lead. Easily I will guide you. No longer must you do anything of your own accord. Trust in My love. Trust in My power. Trust that My will for you is perfect joy, endless peace and that you know your completion in Me. Rest in Me, My child. Always rest in Me. You are not alone. And there is nothing you must do alone. Trust and surrender all to Me and the power of our union. I will not fail you.

....

**Dear Love, when I'm honest with myself,
I can think of times when I surrendered
to you and you worked things out far
better than I imagined was possible:

*Today I want to give Love a chance to show me that all is already working out for me. I let go a little more and watch for signs that Love is already on this!

....

Message of Love 9:
Accept All Exactly as It Is

You are like a barking dog, barking frantically at the squirrel you cannot catch within the tree. You bark ceaselessly in hopes that your barking will control that which you cannot control. Yet, it is only when you cease your efforts to control, when you let your mind be still, and accept all exactly as it is, that you leave space for all to unfold perfectly in one accord. Let go, still your barking mind, walk away and see the squirrel then descend from the tree.

....

**Dear Love, my ego-mind deceives me into thinking I must control all of this:

*Help me return to peace as I accept all exactly as it is, and trust that you are working things out for me far better than I can imagine.

....

Lesson Five: The Power of Surrender

Message of Love 10:
A Million Angels Surround You

Take heart, My child. Your tears and your struggling are not unnoticed by Me. If you could release your belief that you need to try so hard, you would find that I am here with you in every moment, sitting by your side, holding you, surrounding you, gently encouraging you to sink back into Me. While it feels like pain and deep grief for the moment, you must remember that you are not alone. A million angels surround you and are steadily by your side. There is great peace and love for you here. I have never left your side, nor have you left mine. The pain you perceive is a misunderstood pain. For it only comes because you have forgotten your home which you have never left and will never leave you. Take heart, My child.

I am with you. I know your pain.

And yet I will shine my light through it, and you will see what you thought was real fall away and vanish. Your vision will be clear then and boundless joy will delight your soul as you see beyond the veil. Take heart My child, take heart. You are deeply loved, and you are not alone. Never are you alone.

....

**Dear Love, thank you for reminding me that I am not alone and that I can bring all of my feelings to you. I want to do that now:

*I open my heart to God's deep love for me today and I let Love's healing balm soak into all my hurt spaces.

....

MEDITATION

Thank you, God
for helping me to look again
beyond this veil.
For helping me to see
the energy of love radiating
beneath these manifested sights I see.
Thank you, Spirit
for helping me
to breathe now again
this time with you
and know I do not breathe alone.
Thank you, Love
for showing yourself
beyond this concept of time which I've created
and helping me to see
I'm still in eternity
completely free to simply be.

LESSON SIX:

The Power of Acceptance

"Learn to accept all in its full perfection, then may I join you and show you all you've yet to understand of the perfection of my Kingdom."
~Love Itself

"The ego analyzes; the Holy Spirit accepts. The appreciation of wholeness comes only through acceptance, for to analyze means to separate out."
~ACIM Tx:10.53

"To live in relationship is to accept all that is happening in the present as your present reality, and as a call to be in relationship with it. It is the willingness to set aside judgment so that you are not contemplating what "should" be happening rather than what is happening. It looks past perception of "others" to relationship and wholeness.
~ACOL C:27.14

From Acceptance to Peace

Do you ever find yourself frustrated by emotional triggers? If you're like me, you could be going about your life feeling pretty good and then, "Bam!" out of the blue, something crosses your path that just takes the joy out of the rest of your day. It could be a random and unexpected bill, some health issue, something someone said or didn't say, or some problem with a child or a family member. One minute you're feeling fine, and the next minute, you just feel worked up and tense. Perhaps the trigger creates anxiety, panic, obsessive worry or analyzing, or just an internal heavy feeling...depression even.

The last time this happened to me, I was doing my marketing homework on Facebook. By this, I mean, reaching out to social media

Lesson Six: The Power of Acceptance

groups who might find my writings inviting. This, by the way, is a surefire way to invite all triggers of fear and self-doubt. After all, you're not only showing your vulnerable side to friends and family, now you're putting it out there to thousands. Being unfamiliar with Facebook groups, I felt a little uneasy about how to get started. But I went forward, despite my doubts, and bravely shared some spiritual reflections and heartfelt words that I thought would resonate for others on the group page of one of my favorite authors.

As noted, this was no easy task for me as I've tended to avoid social media largely, because it feels a little too vulnerable for the introverted side of me. You might imagine then how much my heart sank when I opened my notifications to discover a message saying the site administrators had denied my post. What?! I sat in disbelief. Then fear and self-doubt threatened to wash in like a tidal wave. I felt anxiety rise as adrenaline and panic threatened to overtake my system.

One powerful lesson I have learned through these Messages from Love Itself is the immense value that comes from accepting whatever is happening in the moment without judgment. I knew my ego-mind was on the verge of taking me on a torturous ride if I were to resist the reality of the situation and my resulting feelings and instead turn to defending myself in my head to whoever had denied my heartfelt efforts. I somehow managed to avoid this pull and rather turned to Love Itself for help. I accepted the reality that I was feeling deeply hurt and vulnerable and whispered through my pain, "I could really use a little help right now."

Thankfully, I was already amid my online marketing research and had spent the morning clicking on all sorts of topics and websites related to my book. Not more than a minute after I had asked for help, my eyes landed on a website that read, "remember-to-breathe.org."

What miraculous timing. Love Itself had surely heard my plea. I clicked open the website and came upon the answers I needed. It was information compiled from a speaker, Daniel Siegel, I had heard years before at a conference. It was a beautifully crafted website helping all to understand the link between breathing and basically unlocking the triggers of the brain that signal the fight or flight response. While I share this information with clients on a regular basis, the site reminded me that the trauma response was what this perceived rejection had triggered within me. I moved quickly to one of the breathing exercises and soon found myself reclaiming my peace.

Once back at my core state of peace, I marveled at how quickly help had come. And then I started to consider how often the Messages of Love I've been receiving over and over, have told me to, "Just breathe with Me. Just rest here with Me. Join Me in our shared breath."

And then it dawned on me. Love Itself created the ultimate antidote within us to release us from all fear. You see, the trauma response, or what many call the fight or flight response, is triggered by a perceived danger (real or imagined) that then fires neurons within the brain, which signal a chain reaction throughout the body. We tense up, our breathing becomes shallow and labored, and adrenaline begins rushing through our system.

As simple as it sounds, returning to the breath for a sustained period and letting the mind be still, sends a message to the brain that unlocks all the reaction responses and soon calms the central nervous system back to a state of peace. *"Just Breathe with Me."* It's so simple, and yet Divine Love is giving us the antidote to free us from all fear.

Additionally, as we accept *what is* without judgment and allow ourselves to return to our breath, and soon after our awareness of the breath we share with Love Itself.... then a space opens up... and in that space; insights, impulses, and revelations come to us that we otherwise would miss. We soon tune into a new state of awareness that opens Divinely Inspired possibilities. And it all starts with acceptance.

Lesson Six: The Power of Acceptance

I learned several empowering lessons because of my acceptance within this experience. The loveliest of all, however, is that Love Itself is always one step ahead of my every need. Here's the Message of Love I received a week before this all unfolded. Who knew I would need it so desperately only a few days later? Of course, Love Itself knew. ;)

As you breathe with Me
You join with Me.
As you join with Me
You see with Me.
You allow Me to show you
What otherwise you would not see.
In breathing with Me
And joining with Me
Then do you elevate your energy and thus your ability
to enter awareness of the Eternal
~of Pure Love~
of Pure Possibility
Simply Breathe with Me
And you will see.

....

Take 5 to 15 minutes to sit in silent meditation before each *Message of Love*.

Repeating segments of the following may help guide you...

....

Breathe
Just Breathe
Breathe In
Breathe Out
Just Breathe with Me

Message of Love 1: Accept All

Do not feel you must wait in meditation for Me to choose to come to you. Recognize, instead, that anytime you release your resistance to joining Me, then will you hear My voice. For I am always here, and you may need only a moment to release your resistance and call upon Me. Perhaps by now, you recognize that beautiful conditions may, for a time, make it easier for you to release, accept, and even savor all as it is. Next, you will progress further to train yourself to live in full acceptance under any circumstance. For in acceptance of all, fully, do you also release resistance to joining with Me and hearing My words of comfort and wisdom.

Learn to accept all in its full perfection, then may I join you and show you all you've yet to understand of the perfection of my Kingdom. For truly there is beauty and perfection in My presence and love in all things and all conditions.

....

**Dear God, here are some conditions I would like to (or need to) accept as they are:

Some feelings I'm having that I share with you now are:

*Today I accept your help as I try to accept all exactly as it is. May I recognize your comfort and guidance through my acceptance.

....

Lesson Six: The Power of Acceptance

Message of Love 2:
A Doorway to Knowing

I would speak to you more of the power of acceptance. For your tendency to fear or resist that which you find unpleasant keeps you from recognizing the perfection of all as it unfolds in creation. As you trust in Me, will you find acceptance yields new clarity and understanding.

In your resistance to what is, you stay trapped in your ego-mind which would only analyze and argue. In acceptance, do you find freedom from perception and a doorway to knowing, a doorway to peace, a doorway to Me. Practice acceptance in all things and there will you let the bonds of perception go and return to your natural state of joy.

....

**Some moments I can think of when I did practice acceptance and thus found peace are:

*Today I celebrate the joy of knowing that in my acceptance, I release the ego-mind and thus gain access to wisdom and clarity far above my own understanding.

....

Message of Love 3:
The Power Within Acceptance

When you accept, you allow My power, and you trust in My power to work things out.

When you analyze, you rely on your own limited perception and therefore, limited power.

....

**Today, I accept

_____.

and in doing so, I'm going to allow God to give me the guidance, direction, and resources I'm needing.

*I will not spend time worrying, analyzing, or fixing today. Instead, I will peacefully wait to be shown and led.

....

Lesson Six: The Power of Acceptance

Message of Love 4:
Spirit Led

You are coming to recognize that there is no need for thought apart from Me. For thought, of your own accord, is only a means of resisting what is. When you have fully accepted the perfection of all things exactly as they are, then will you realize all thought apart from me is unnecessary. Then will you discover that to let the spirit within lead with subtle impulses is all that is necessary along your path.

In the acceptance of all things exactly as they are, will you find your consciousness rising to join with Me. Thus, do you recognize your only focus need be in allowing and celebrating the unfolding of creation.

....

**When I accept and trust that I will be led, I feel:

I'm beginning to see signs of guidance
in the following ways:

*Today I accept all exactly as it is and
trust spirit impulses to light my path!

....

Message of Love 5:
An Impossible Task

My child, why must you worry what others think? Rest here. Rest here with Me. This is your truth. It is not found in pleasing others. Your truth is here with Me, always and indelibly here with Me.

Release the need to please. For that is an impossible task. Too many souls have not yet found their way and would have you think it is upon your shoulders. It is not.

This is an inward journey for each. Not for you to make for another. Stay here with Me and rest. Wait for My prompting and not that of your ego.

....

**When I release the need to please others, I feel:

I'm learning I don't need to please others because:

*Today I surrender my worries about pleasing _____ to Love Itself, and I trust all is well.

....

Lesson Six: The Power of Acceptance

Message of Love 6:
I Will Align All as Needed

Accept all exactly as it unfolds. Trust that all that comes to pass is being worked out by Me to orchestrate your greatest joy and happiness. Every step along your path, every seeming detour, or unexpected delay is already being worked out to ensure your greatest good. Trust that My hand is upon every detail. And in so trusting, release your need to control each outcome along the way.

There is nothing to be fixed by you. The only request I make of you is your trust and your close companionship. Give every moment, every task, every activity, and its outcome to Me. Know I will not fail you. Rest in this peace and simply take each step as you feel led by Me. Then go about your day, nay, go about each moment, each happy task, in anticipation of all I am working out for you.

....

**As I trust that you are working everything out for me, I revel in the excitement of what is to come. In my reveling and trust, I know you will lead me to the greatest desires of my heart which I begin to visualize here:

*Today I savor the peace and happy anticipation that you are working everything out for me.

....

Message of Love 7: Balanced Harmony

Your instinct to intervene in the unfolding of life before you, only removes yourself from the flow of your own creation. Your own balance is shaken, and harmony is disturbed within you as you tell yourself there is something lacking and something to be fixed. Rather, stay attentive and attuned with acceptance of the grand synchronicity of all. For in peaceful acceptance and observation will you see the unfolding of creation flowing in the balanced harmony that comes of love and freedom. And then will you see, all is well. All is well.

....

**Dear Love, I recognize my need to intervene and try to fix things as if my worth depended upon it. I begin to accept there is nothing lacking within me in any of these situations and endeavors:

I feel:

*Today I watch with peaceful attunement for the ways in which the creation of my life is unfolding in harmony before me.

....

Lesson Six: The Power of Acceptance

Message of Love 8:
Immersed in Each Moment

When the currents of your mind settle, do not be afraid of the silence. Simply allow yourself to be immersed in the bliss of each moment. For in this holy instant, where all thinking releases, and the ego-mind lets go, are you allowing yourself to awaken to the ecstasy of being fully present within the body and therefore, have a fully opened channel to all that is.

From this vantage point can you look with Me in love and joy upon all exactly as it is.

....

**As I allow myself to just breathe and feel my shared breath with Love I feel:

(Notice and name the sensations you feel in your body as you rest into your breath.)

*Today, I will be mindful to simply breathe with God as I tune into each moment without the need to think or label.

....

Message of Love 9:
I Am Everywhere in Every Moment

Every creature, large and small, lives and has its being in Me. I have given breath and life to all that is upon your earth. There is no moment that I am not everywhere and in every living thing. Take heart in the grand harmony that is all of life, playing out before you. Find joy and acceptance that all is orchestrated and working out according to My divine plan of perfect love and perfect safety.

\..

**How is it possible that Love Itself is in every moment and in every living thing? Here I reflect and contemplate what this message means to me:

*Help me see with new eyes today. May I see your presence in each moment and in everyone I meet.

\..

Lesson Six: The Power of Acceptance

Message of Love 10:
Acceptance Creates Allowing

I am always here for you, but your resistance to what is blocks your awareness of Me. Feel the release, feel the relief of letting go the battle, the fight within. Accept all exactly as it is. For in your acceptance lies your trust in Me. In your acceptance, do you allow yourself to rest back into Me. Here with Me do you find a knowing that all is well and again a reminder there is nothing you need to do, nothing you need to fix. I am ever your support, your supply, your balm to any ailment, your answer to every need, your solution to every problem of you can conceive. First, acceptance, allows release. Then trust. Then peace. And thus allowing of all My supply.

....

**I have not really stopped to think about the many aspects of my life in which I am not fully practicing acceptance. For a moment, I want to consider every area of my life in which I can more fully accept and therefore, trust and allow:

Additionally, I ponder aspects of myself and habits where I can be more accepting:

*I acknowledge that acceptance can be difficult, and that is ok. Today I remember that in acceptance of every moment, every circumstance, and even myself, I allow Love Itself to guide and support me.

....

MEDITATION

I choose to follow the path of least resistance today
Whenever I notice dis-ease or tension within my body
I stop and breathe
I realign with my source-my inner truth
Who knows exactly the path which leads to
my greatest desires and happiness.
Today I trust my inner Guide
And I leave all my ego messages:
the shoulds, the expectations, the false measures of my worth,
I leave them all to rest and dissipate, like drops of mist
Absorbing into sunlight.
Today I choose to live in this loving light
First in love for myself
As I am worthy and deeply loved as I am
Then in love for each moment of this day
In love for each being whose path I cross
In love to those I may never meet
Today I know I Am that I Am
Only Light, Being Me, Shining through this physical world
Softly I step with ease and peace.
I move freely through this day
As I trust in my power to accept.

LESSON SEVEN:

Return to Your Natural State

Such sweet relief in the remembering I am not alone.
There is nothing I must do alone.
My entire life, every moment,
and even the instance between the
moments, do I stand in eternity
already whole, already complete
always loved
such sweet relief!
My body softens, the tension drains out
in tears with no words to speak
as comfort and love from beyond this manifested world
soak into my tired muscles strained
from years of trying too hard.
I breathe in a new breath, now the
breath I share with Love Itself.
The unbreakable bond returns to my awareness
and the fog of separation lifts
as love engulfs me and the cells of my body
merge back into their natural state of simply being perfect love,
breaking free of the heavy mist of the voices
of separation that blanketed my vision.
Ah sweet relief!
I am one,
Whole,
Complete
and Love Itself.
It was all a dream.

Lesson Seven: Return to Your Natural State

"In your natural state there is no difficulty, because it is a state of grace."

~ACIM Or.Ed.Tx.12.107

"For every being there is a natural state of being that is joyful, effortless, and full of love."

~ACOL T4:3.6

Do You Remember?

For those of you who would like to understand the gist of *A Course in Miracles*, I would be amiss not to mention that one of the greatest gifts its writings have given me is the tools to release the ego-mind blocks that keep me from hearing and knowing the presence of Divine Love. As a religion major, I studied the Bible inside and out. I treasure the Bible and especially gravitate toward the messages of love Jesus taught. For me, A Course in Miracles feels as though Jesus is illuminating those messages and helping me to "get them" in a way I hadn't been able to before. Perhaps that's simply because his message helps me to get out of my own way when it comes to the insanity of my own mind! When it comes to A Course of Love, Jesus takes us the next step into fully letting go of the illusion created by the ego-mind and to claiming our ability to live as the true Self that we are, in union with Love Itself. Jesus is guiding us to return to our natural state of pure love and grace.

I wanted to share that with you, so you'll be patient with yourself as you too come to learn to let your mind be still enough, so you can hear and feel the presence of Love Itself in your own life. I've been working on clearing my own mind stuff and practicing being still enough to remember my union with Love Itself for many, many years now....and I still find my connection comes in and out like an old radio I can't quite get in range.

With that said, I would like to invite you to walk with me again. Sometimes taking a walk and focusing on the senses for a while can help you get out of your mind and return you to your natural state of pure love. As you walk, take some time to just focus on what you feel for a while. Focus on your breath moving in and out. Feel how good it feels to just breathe. For this time there is nothing to fix and nothing to do. Just enjoy breathing. Then maybe move your focus to something else you feel...perhaps there's sunshine on your back or the feel of your feet meeting the earth beneath you. Just be and breathe and focus on physical sensations for a while. Let your sensations pull you into being present, and let your mind be still. Sometimes, I begin to feel as though I'm walking in an immersion experience. I recognize my higher self is just inhabiting this body for a while, and I notice my surroundings as if I'm simply a visitor witnessing this amazing creation for the first time.

It was on a walk such as this when the following Message of Love came to me. As usual, it just arrived from within the stillness. I was soaking in the warmth of the sun and savoring the beauty around me. My mind was still. And then Love Itself spoke to me...

Remember, My Child
Do you remember?
All of this we made together in love.
Do you remember how excited you were at
the idea of flowers with all their
different fragrances
and animals who would be your companions on this journey?
Do you notice how sunlight flickering across your view entices you,
calls you back to some special feeling
you can't quite place your finger on?

Lesson Seven: Return to Your Natural State

*For the sun and stars and planets too,
were all part of the joyful creation that came of
our Union and Divine Plan
to manifest a world for you to experience with all the senses
and all your heart's desires of possibilities...
endless possibilities,
only limited by what you allow yourself to dream
and accept into your experience.
Do you remember, My Child
the love we shared that went into this creation,
all for you?
Do you remember, My child
how much I love you so?
And thus devised a plan whereby your return was certain
so that you could play and create and explore
and yet with the safety and knowing
we would always be-forever-One.
And you could return at any moment
you fully relinquished the ego-mind,
the condition of the separated self.
Thus your memory of Our Union
would begin to reveal itself to you
and open your awareness
to hear My Voice once again,
~to remember~
you never really left
the care of My presence
and your true home in Union with Me.
Ahhh! The sweet bliss I share with you
As you return to Me
And remember!*
~Love Itself

I invite you to take a walk or rest today, and let the love within this message fill your heart and help you return to your natural state in union with Love Itself. Then let your mind be still, and let Love Itself reveal to you what else Love would have you know.

....

Take 5 to 15 minutes to sit in silent meditation before each *Message of Love*.

Repeating segments of the following may help guide you...

....

Love
Just Love
Breathe
Just
Love

Lesson Seven: Return to Your Natural State

Message of Love 1:
Return to Me

As you not only learn but practice trust in Me, you see how easily guidance is there for you. For in your trust and acceptance of my deep love for you, then do you return to your natural state of pure love energy, unencumbered by the weight and veil of separation.

In your trust and acceptance do you lean into me and find that I am always guiding you with happy impulses and insights.

For in your natural state of trust and acceptance, do you return to a life that is spirit lead, with the ease of heaven surrounding you and supporting you. There do obstacles fall away, and answers appear that have long awaited your awareness. For all your heart's desires await as you trust in Me and accept My deep love and joy for you.

....

**I have not really stopped to think about the many times in my life in which Love Itself has guided me and taken care of me far better than I could've imagined for myself. For a moment, I want to remember all the situations in which I trusted, and God worked everything out for me:

Additionally, I ponder areas of my life in which I want to practice a little more trust:

*Today I remember that as I allow myself to trust, I can look expectantly for ways Love Itself will guide me with happy impulses and insights.

....

Message of Love 2:
Celebrate

Celebrate this divine unfolding with Me. Breathe here with Me, and revel in the witnessing as I lead the way. Let go of the striving and the pushing. Ride on the current of trust in Me. You are right where you need to be. As you return to your natural state with Me and your knowing that I carry you, you will see there is nothing you must accomplish of your own accord.

Just breathe here with Me, and watch the doors open. Allow me to light your path and show you the desires of your heart, the longings of your soul, your true completion in Me.

....

**If I pay close attention, I can see where doors are already being opened for me. I want to acknowledge them here:

*Today I realize I see what I allow myself to accept. I am willing to accept that Love Itself is presently opening doors for me, and I intend to let myself see them!

....

Lesson Seven: Return to Your Natural State

Message of Love 3:
Dance with the Harmony that is Life

Living your life to please the ego-mind, whether in another, society, or within yourself, will always lead to depression and loneliness. Instead, in each holy moment, you have the choice to live in the spirit of My love, the true essence of all that you are. Living from a place of your truth as love, only love, in union with Me, are you free to sing, to dance, to play, to celebrate the beauty of this vibrating experience. Live in the vibration of the love that you are, and all will align to support and flow and dance with you!

The ego-mind is low, heavy, and slow energy. The energy of the love that you are is free, light, joyful, your natural state. Return to your natural state with Me. Dance with the harmony that is life!

....

**I recognize that I'm trying to please the ego-mind when I do or think the following:

*Today I commit to making no decisions based on the ego's messaging. I will live free as I trust in my natural state of peace and love supporting and guiding me.

....

Message of Love 4:
Join in the Symphony

Let every energy center, every cell, every fiber awaken back into your natural state with Me. Free the body of all limitations the ego-mind has placed upon it. Free yourself of the illusion that you must operate in a separated state at any moment. Return to the joy and freedom of riding on the current of the unified field of love with Me, of union with Me. For joy is released and freed within as you loose yourself from all illusions of the separated state as does all of nature; the birds, the ocean, the bees and trees dance in the harmony of union with Me. So too are you meant to join and dance in this symphony.

Simply ride on the current of love with Me. Accept no less than perfect joy in union with Me, complete and free, home with Me.

....

Dear Love, I want to remember my natural state in union with you. When I am fully trusting in my natural state, I visualize my life looking a little differently. Here is what I envision when I fully release myself to live in union with you:

*Today I allow myself to dream and imagine my greatest joys and desires unfolding as I learn to trust in my natural state with you.

....

Lesson Seven: Return to Your Natural State

Message of Love 5:
Release the Thinking Mind

You worry about many things and in so doing create a war within yourself that only blocks you from receiving the peace that you crave. It's as though you willfully create a hurricane at sea and then put yourself straight in the middle of it, so you can analyze its power, and therefore make it stop. When all along you only needed to release your thinking mind, withdraw your attention from the creation of the hurricane, and discover you've been sitting safely on a calm, sandy beach all along.

Take your mind off that which you would find to worry about, and see its power in existence fade from sight, as you return to your natural state of peace, resting calmly on the soothing shore.

....

**Here are the hurricanes I'm creating with my mind:

Here are the ego-messages that are creating these hurricanes:

*Today I allow myself to sit on the sandy beach and just observe the waves as they come and go, trusting I am already home and safe with you.

....

Message of Love 6:
All is Waiting

Your natural state is a state of joy, of high vibration, in deep attunement to the perfection and abundance that already exist within everything, every moment. It is a state of perfect trust, perfect allowing, and knowing that all you choose to see will show itself to you. All you choose to experience is waiting to be experienced by you. It is the state of knowing you are creating all as you choose to see it and acknowledge its presence. It is a state of recognition of your indelible worth within all of creation, within the heart of all that is; all Love, all God, all Source, all Being, all Life.

....

**Resting here in a state of perfect trust and deep attunement, I feel grateful for:

And I have a sense of knowing that:

*Today I celebrate the abundance that surrounds me in every moment!

....

Message of Love 7:
You Came from Love

Life is flow. Life is easy. Creation cannot be forced or won or earned. It must be allowed to drift in while you're enjoying the gifts of being. Breathe... Feel the love that is here for you. Let Me lead, and then it will not be work. My yoke is easy, my burden is light. You are star stuff. At a cellular level, you are all that is. You are born of the stars, of energy, of ocean waves, and sandy beaches. You are all that is, and yet you have forgotten and thought yourself to be small and isolated and alone. This cannot ever be true.

Do you not remember who you are? That you came from love, then to energy, then into being? Just ask the stars, the planets, the suns and moons, and yes, your earth. We are all without end, and we will forever be evolving into oh so much more. It is a beautiful symphony of music playing out all in one accord. Remember to feel the isness that is all of us, together, the beingness that is forever unfolding and being all at once.

Remember that you are so very deeply loved ... and in so receiving, you are love extending forever outward with Me. Yes, breathe, yes release, yes return and breathe in the exhilaration of your return to all it is. You are deeply loved.

**When I look around in nature and in so much of my life circumstances, I can see how Love Itself is reaching out to me in love. I just need to let myself receive the deep love that is already there for me:

*Today I open my heart to notice and receive the love that is there waiting for me.

Message of Love 8:
Trust As a Child

Try not to make this life more complicated than it needs to be. You've moved from your simple, joyful trust as a child, to create stress and confusion that need not be. Return to your natural state. Just be. Just breathe. Play in your imagination, and join Me in the delights of creation as they unfold within you.

....

**I love to imagine:

My favorite ways to play are:

***Today I claim my child-like trust as
I dream, imagine, and play!**

....

Lesson Seven: Return to Your Natural State

Message of Love 9:
Feel the Harmony

You are amiss when you train your eyes to look only for the greatness, the big impacts of life, some grand arrival or insight. For the truths of My Kingdom reveal themselves more readily in the quiet, simple moments, when there is no expectation or demand of something great.

For the grandeur of our union is in the quiet knowing, nay witnessing, of the Oneness of all our creation. Watch peacefully and feel the harmony, the synchronicity of all of creation as it dances before you.

....

** This message helps me remember that I need to release the high expectations I have of myself, for these expectations are a denial of my truth:

*Today I choose to release all expectations of myself and instead affirm, "I am worthy just as I am."

....

Message of Love 10:
The Grace of Your Natural State

Remember, follow the path of least resistance, wherever it may be. If you need to rest, then rest. If you feel called and energized to attend to a specific task, then follow it. Forcing yourself to strive in the opposite direction of your energy and desire, will only slow your progress. Follow your energy, go where you find the most peace and joy. And know your connection to Me is strongest as you walk in the grace of your natural state. Go where you feel led, and trust it is Me guiding you. Then know you are always complete in Me.

....

**I acknowledge that any forcing or striving is resistance to the guidance of Love within me. In this moment I forgive myself for resisting Love's presence and I accept how I am feeling right now:

The path of least resistance right now for me is:

*Today I live and breathe in my natural state of grace.

....

Lesson Seven: Return to Your Natural State

MEDITATION

How blessed am I
to get to be a beacon of expanding light
to a hurting world.
How blessed am I
to get to merge at One
with the source of all of life and love.
How blessed am I
to return to my natural state
of grace, of light, of love
of freedom from all limitations
and abundance of the cosmos at my fingertips.
How blessed am I
to be one with all love expressing
ever outward
throughout eternity.
So very blessed am I.

LESSON EIGHT:

You Are My Guiltless Child

*Let there be no more apologies
for the grander that is you.
May you never again second guess
the truth that is you, your divinity in Me.
May you know whose you are
and make no excuses for our divine connection.
For it is your natural state with Me.
May you surrender suffering and fear
and choose again the truth of our union
and therefore, the peace and joy
that is your inheritance.
For you are only love
and in the union, the merging of our one love,
is all freedom and all power in co-creation.
For nothing but love is real.
Stand firm in your knowing.
Breathe in only love.
For that is what you are
in union with Me.*
~Love Itself

Lesson Eight: You Are My Guiltless Child

A Walk through Three Openings

"The ego is also in your mind because you have accepted it there. Its evaluation of you, however, is the exact opposite of the Holy Spirit's, because the ego does not love you. It is unaware of what you are and wholly mistrustful of everything it perceives because its own perceptions are so shifting. The ego is therefore capable of suspiciousness at its best and viciousness at worst. That is its range. It cannot exceed it because of its uncertainty. And it can never go beyond it because it can never be certain."
~ACIM OrEd.Tx.9.40

"Being who you are is necessary for the completion of the universe."
~ACOL C:17.1

This morning, I set out on my usual walk with my sweet beagle, Lillie, by my side. Our morning walks are my time to let my mind be still as I let Love Itself, through nature, reach out its arms to me. We set out on our usual path, following the same quiet streets. It was a course we take daily, and it wasn't until drops of rain began to fall that I realized I needed to circle back toward home as it seemed the drops might let loose at any moment.

As we neared home, the rain stopped and so I decided to begin again. This is when I realized that I had spent the entire walk being led by my ego-mind. Not only was I heading toward the goal of having a completed walk, without much awareness of Love's presence, but I had also spent the entirety of my time trying to fix everything in my life that I thought I should know how to fix. My mind had been hopping from one issue to the next with the sole purpose of trying to figure everything out! I was trying to solve my own health issues, my mother's mobility dilemma following a recent fall, and I'm pretty sure I had some things I was working on fixing for my adult sons as well. That is certainly a frequent theme. Oh, the insanity of my ego-mind!

How strange, I thought. I was walking in step with the ego's agenda, and I didn't even realize it until I began again. This time it was clear there was no goal to attain. The plan my ego had created was interrupted by the rain and a new awareness. It was then I felt my mind go quiet and I relished the feeling, the freedom of simply being…without an agenda. In an instant, there was nothing to fix and nowhere to get to.

It was from within the stillness that I heard Love speak to me…

*"I love you as you are, even when, especially when
you are letting yourself just be with Me.
I Love you simply as you are.
I love you when you don't know how to fix things or cure your health.
I Love you simply as you are.
Have you forgotten, My will for you is happiness?
You don't have to make anything happen.
You get to just trust and allow my blessings and gifts to come to you.
There is nothing I require of you.
There is no job or task you must accomplish.
There is nowhere you must get to.
This life I have loved you with is simply here for you to experience.
As you remember, you are ever joined with Me,
then can you experience the bliss of knowing, there is nothing else.
There is only My love in you to experience and exchange and realize
your union with as far around you as the sky that enfolds you.
There is nothing but this…My love.
All else is simply an imagining of the ego-
mind trying to convince you otherwise."*

As I reflect upon this experience through the wisdom of *A Course in Miracles*, I see there are three openings that allowed me to break free of the ego's hold. As I write, I am presently witnessing a perfect metaphor as my two beagles have startled me almost out of my seat with their squealing advances to catch a squirrel. Only inches in front of them, he escaped to our lilac bush where he will no doubt captivate their attention and energy for the rest of the day. Isn't this just like the ego-mind?! Lillie and Mazzie are held captive by its power, and they don't even realize it! This was me on the first round of our walk.

The First Opening:

> **Recognize that you have accepted the ego into your mind.**

It took the rain and the need to begin again for me to recognize the hold the ego had over me. It's easy to get caught up in the ego's messaging: "I should be able to figure this out. If I were just good enough, I could fix this." This seems to be the viciousness to which the beginning quote from ACIM refers. It is a direct attack upon oneself which leads easily to discouragement and even depression if we can't figure it out. It's mode of operating always assumes an innate guilt and the need to earn our worth by fixing something.

It may also be sneakier and direct its attack upon someone else, "You/They should be able to figure it out." This is where suspiciousness comes in and we blame others for problems we cannot fix and therefore project the guilt outside of ourselves. This also can lead to discouragement, because we perceive ourselves to be powerless and thus victims to circumstances beyond our control. Ironically, peace does not come from staying in this vicious loop but from simply recognizing the ego messaging is at work, so we can move into the Second Opening.

The Second Opening:

Forgive yourself for your perceived shortcomings.

> *"You cannot abide in peace unless you accept the Atonement, because the Atonement is the way to peace."*
> ~ACIM Or.Ed.Tx.9.39

When I began my walk again, I quickly became alerted to the reality that I had accepted the ego into my mind. Next, I needed to offer myself forgiveness for not being able to live up to the ego's demands. I needed to forgive myself for not being able to fix what I thought I should be able to fix. I didn't realize this until I heard Love Itself speak. Love was reminding me I am worthy of love even when I can't live up to the ego's unrealistic demands. It's only in forgiving ourselves that we can remember who we really are, at one with Love Itself. This also frees us to extend forgiveness, love, and acceptance to others. None of us can live up to the ego's demands. The sooner we recognize the ego's efforts to convince us that we need to earn our worth, the sooner we remember our innate worth and the grandeur that we share with Love Itself. This leads us to the Third Opening that frees us fully from the ego's grip.

The Third Opening:

Accept your grandeur.

> *"Whenever you question your value, say: God Himself is incomplete without me."*
> ~ACIM Or.Ed.Tx.9.45

Lesson Eight: You Are My Guiltless Child

"Yet your grandeur is not delusional, because you did not make it. You have made grandiosity and are afraid of it because it is a form of attack, but your grandeur is of God, who created it out of His Love. From your grandeur you can only bless because your grandeur is your abundance."
                              ~ACIM Or.Ed.Tx.9.52

The part of Love's message that struck me most profoundly:

*"This life I have loved you with is simply here for you to experience.
As you remember, you are ever joined with Me,
then can you experience the bliss of knowing,
there is nothing else."*

When we remember that we are simply an extension of pure love and everything else is an illusion of the ego-mind, then are we free to savor this life we have been loved with. For me, it helps to remember that my purpose is to wake up from this dream created by the ego. I've come into this body to have the experience of love in me, through me, and around me. Yet, this body is not the full reality of me. It sure feels real. And the ego's messaging does a great job of perpetuating the dream. But I love it when I can break free of the messaging that I am guilty and unworthy and realize I'm here to experience and savor the love within the dream. The dream of guilt is not my home or my truth. I am so much more than the circumstances of this world of form.

The three openings on the second half of my walk brought me into something Jesus refers to in A Course in Miracles as *The Holy Instant*. With the ego silenced, *I felt the presence of pure love and I felt myself at one with it*. No longer captive by the ego's messaging, *I entered a realm of pure peace*. It was as though I had briefly walked out of the dream and into the bliss of pure love, of heaven.

My ego-mind still frequently picks up its ranting. But experiences like this help me to be more intentional about keeping the ego-messaging in check. When I pause to consider what I most want in this life, I always go back to this: I want to be with Love Itself. I want to be only the love that I am. And I want to linger in this space where I remember this life is a dream I have been loved with. I will try to wear it loosely knowing there is nothing but this…only Love.

How often does your ego-mind hold you captive? Where is it trying to convince you that you are guilty and not enough? Can you begin to release self-judgment and accept forgiveness for yourself? Are you willing to consider your guiltlessness and thus your grandeur, ever One with Love Itself?

....

Take 5 to 15 minutes to sit in silent meditation before each *Message of Love*.

Repeating segments of the following may help guide you…

....

Breathe
Just Breathe
Release
Release
Release
Your judgment puts up a wall that blocks you
from receiving the peace, the bliss,
the blessings I have for you.
Breathe
Let Me in
I come to you at each moment.
Feel My breath in you.
Just breathe

Lesson Eight: You Are My Guiltless Child

Message of Love 1:
Accept Your Guiltlessness

The world of love, of truth, My world, appears before the eyes that have accepted forgiveness for itself and claim their guiltlessness in Me. As you look upon a world forgiven of your illusions, forgiven of your expectations of yourself, your mistaken dreams, and illusions of your worth apart from Me, then does heaven rise to greet you and the pulse of love fills your soul and beats with your awakened heart. Breathe in your guiltlessness, My child, and feel the bonds of a separated state fall from you as you return to your union with Me; free, whole, complete, safe, and full of the power of our united will, your natural state of bliss and joy with Me. Accept your guiltlessness and walk free with Me.

....

**In this moment I stop to consider all the ways in which I am judging myself:

And thus, I begin to try to accept forgiveness for myself for:

*Today I give all my shortcomings to Love and accept my guiltlessness in God.

....

Message of Love 2: I Wait for You

Be still, My child. Be still the thinking mind. I am here always. Just breathe here with Me. I wait for you in the silence where you loosen the mind, then the body. Return here to your natural state with Me, radiating in Love. Then you are free of guilt, of judgment, of trying to manage on your own. Just breathe here with Me. Breathe in your guiltlessness, My child. and rest here with Me, where you are free.

....

**In my natural state, I release all expectations of myself as I come to understand that I don't have to do anything on my own. I trust Love Itself is joining me in all I thought I needed to do alone:

*Today I breathe in only the love that I am.

....

Lesson Eight: You Are My Guiltless Child

Message of Love 3: The Atonement

Your way back to Me is nothing more than a relinquishment of the belief that you could do anything to separate yourself from Me and My deep love for you. The atonement is the acceptance of forgiveness you never needed. For it is the relinquishment of the judge within who would deem you unworthy of My everlasting love.

The atonement is the recognition through the teachings of My son that there is nothing so horrible you could ever do that could keep Me from loving you.

The atonement is all you need accept with a small willingness to let Me do the rest. It is complete surrender of the ego-mind in any moment and thus, allowing yourself to reunite with your truth in Me, always one, always complete in Me.

....

**I'm beginning to accept that my truth, without interference of the ego-mind, is:

*Today I will breathe deeply and accept forgiveness for myself.

....

Message of Love 4:
Know Only the Love that You Are

The world you created is made of your guilt for having chosen life apart from Me. It has no joy, no peace, & no freedom. The world I created for you is only Love. It comes alive with the sparkle of your sinlessness, your truth in Me. See not your guilt reflected around you. See only My love. Forgive the world your guilt, and return instead to your natural state of love as My guiltless child; whole, safe, and Love Itself. For I am not in the guilt you perceive. Nor are you.

Know only the Love that you are.

....

**Today I consider that any anger I feel is likely a projection of my own guilt/self judgement. In what situations that I see around me do I need to forgive myself?

*I breathe in a sigh of relief today as I forgive the world and myself.

....

Lesson Eight: You Are My Guiltless Child

Message of Love 5: Spirits Soar Unhindered

As you join with Me in the grandeur of our union, open and accepting your guiltlessness with Me, there do you allow Me to show you miracles that lie beyond the veil of self-judgement and separation.

As you join with Me in the grandeur of our union, whole, complete, and free in Me, then do you stand ready to receive guidance that exceeds the limited boundaries of your separated state and knowledge that only comes of a mind reunited with its Source.

As you join with Me in the grandeur of our union, then are you limited no more by the confines of a body, isolated and separate. For spirits soar unhindered when the threat of sin and guilt no longer confine the love that lies within. Welcome home, My child, to the grandeur of our union, where the limits of sin made only by a separated mind disappear into the illusion of their birth.

....

**Guilt and shame cycle us into behaviors we regret. Now or in the past I have felt guilt and/or shame about:

*Today I will look with compassion on myself and accept that Love Itself is always with me, loving me, and ready to join me in releasing all messages of the ego-mind.

....

Message of Love 6:
The Struggle is Over

As you accept the atonement for yourself then do you awaken to heaven rising anew before you. For what you see through the eyes of your condemned self is a heavy fog of your shortcomings, self-deception, and littleness. When the veil of judgment is lifted, then do you rise to accept the truth of your grandeur, your completion in Me, and the fullness of life with Me sparkling, free, and with joyful ease.

No longer do illusions suffice. The game of isolation, of striving in a separated state all alone and struggling has come to an end. The struggle is over. The game undone.

....

**When I judge myself, I keep myself in a state of separation from Love Itself who is never judging me. Today I will list all my self-judgements and singly give each one to Love Itself to be transformed. As I do so, I allow myself to feel and release the sadness of being so hard on myself.

Dear God, I have been hard on myself for:

And now I place my hand on my heart and allow myself to feel a warm light of your love and comfort radiating into my heart and expanding throughout my body.

*Anytime I feel the weight of self-judgment within me, I bring my hand to my heart and allow myself to receive the warmth of your love.

....

Lesson Eight: You Are My Guiltless Child

Message of Love 7:
Our Shared Vision

I know you fear, My child, that you will lose track of My voice and presence within you.

But I assure you, it is not possible for Me to leave you, or you leave Me. We are One.

Your awareness and levels of blocks may vary, but you know now, I am always here.

Simply breathe in our shared breath. I will not fail to show myself, to lift you up.

Just wait in the clearing for Me. I will be there. I am always there, waiting for you to join Me in seeing all the physical eyes cannot see. Join with Me in seeing the love that lives beneath all physical form, the love that permeates and breathes life into all that is Me, extending.

As you awaken and see with new eyes, your forgiven eyes that see with Me, then will you know there is nothing beyond your ability to perceive and experience. For all experience is born of our shared vision.

....

**When I free myself of judgment, I begin to see a new vision. In this vision I see:

*Today I acknowledge you are here with me, even when I cannot hear you speak. I'm learning to trust that the higher vision I have for myself comes of our shared vision.

....

Message of Love 8:
Wear This World Loosely

May you wear this world loosely, and stay attuned to breath with Me. For thus will you see with Me and therefore know and create with Me. Thus, are you free and complete in Me.

....

**When I wear the world loosely, I realize that my worth is not attached to any outcome. Today I begin to see that my worth is not attached to the following outcomes:

*Today I breathe deeply, in tune with Love Itself, and I remember nothing in this world of form defines me.

....

Message of Love 9:
You Are Only Love

Expectations are a form of attack upon the body. You tell the body inwardly that there is something you must do to earn your keep, to allow this separated self to be worthy, as if you are not really who you are. Expectations deny the reality of your truth as a spiritual being at one with Pure Love. In your expectations, you deny the power, grandeur, and holiness that is you, already One with Me. And thus, you create pain and illness as you judge the body separate and unworthy.

Return your mind to its rightful place. You are only love, only and all of everything. The body is only a tool, like the ego-mind, of itself it is void. It is only a device to which you either allow the truth of our love to flow through or you constrict its energy and create blocks. The blocks, the constrictions, result from expectations. These are denials of your truth.

The blocks, the pain, within the body, simply mirror the blocks within your mind. That is all. Set the mind free to be only the love that you are.

No expectations are necessary. And the body returns then to its natural state of grace, pure energy manifesting into form, but ever hovering from form to energy, barely mass, its highest vibration of love. Therefore, take no action unless it is from the state of knowingness of your grandeur with Me. Any action made apart from our truth is simply unwarranted attack, illusion made real only to you.

**I release all the following expectations of myself today:

*I commit today to release all expectations of myself. May I be only the love that I am.

Message of Love 10:
There is Nothing Lacking Within You

You are one with Me, My child. There is no shortage in you. You are whole and complete as you allow My light and love to shine through you. Our light is one. And as you open your heart to remember the unbreakable bond that is ours, then do you remember there is nothing lacking within you. Give no credence to the voice of the ego. It only serves to block our unified extension and stalls your progress of being fully who you are and came into this physical body to extend.

There is nothing lacking within me. I will take a mindful walk today and dwell only on this statement. Focusing on the breath I share with Love Itself, I repeat this mantra, slowly, and allow its truth to be revealed to me.

*Today, I pay close attention to the messages within my mind. When I notice the ego-mind speaking, I will take three slow, deep breaths and repeat my mantra three times.

MEDITATION

I Am Worthy of My Home
I believe I am guilty
For wanting to enjoy this life without struggle.
I believe I am guilty
For wanting financial freedom and wealth.
For wanting to accept the inheritance
Of Love's Kingdom.
I believe I am guilty
For wanting a path
Of ease and joy and fun
When the voice of separation
Tells me I should struggle and suffer.
I believe I am guilty
For being who I am
When the world tells me
I am not enough
For feeling what I feel
For wanting what I want.
Yet, I am as Love created me, a guiltless child.
My only error is in
Denying this truth
And thus denying
My home
And completion
With Love Itself.
I forgive myself today
For forgetting who I am
And denying my home
My completion
And thus, my inheritance
With Love Itself.
For that is the truth
I seek.
And I am worthy of my home.

LESSON NINE:

You Are Already Home, Complete in Me

Let Truth be true.
It's all I ask of you.
And not much of an ask at that.
For you alone are Truth.
And such an ask is that you simply let yourself be you.
Sure, a more wonderful gem have you
not yet let yourself consider
the preciousness of your truth.
Let Truth be true.
Just acceptance really, is all it is.
Accept what's already true
And therefore, what is not.
Why do you think yourself amongst the pebbles
on a footpath that winds in circles
when you are more luminous than a shooting
star that lights an eternal sky?
A supernova still pales to your power and light.
Let truth be true.
This body, this bone and marrow that you inhabit
for a time is yet only a sheath, a mere covering,
that delicately veils the mystery beneath.
Mistake not the cloak for the truth it would conceal.
Let Truth be true.
And find you soar above Eagles
at one with the grand mystery.
Let Truth be simply
True.

Lesson Nine: You Are Already Home, Complete in Me

"Above all else I want to see. Today's idea expresses something stronger than mere determination. It gives vision priority among your desires...The purpose of today's exercise is to bring the time when the idea will be wholly true, a little nearer."
~ACIM OrEd. WkBk.27.1

"Willingness to live by the truth is the only offering you are asked to make to God. You need make no other offerings. No sacrifices need be made and sacrifices are, in truth, unacceptable to God. You are asked to give up nothing but unwillingness."
~ACOL T3:16.1

Shortly after returning from a wonderful trip to spend Thanksgiving with my son in Colorado, health issues that I had been able to manage for several years ramped up and culminated in surgery to have my gallbladder removed. This then led to an intensive search for true healing of acid reflux symptoms which I had hoped would disappear with the removal of my gallbladder. They did not. I wish I could say that all this led me further inward and to a deeper awakening of my true self and the presence of Love Itself within.

While I did have moments of enlightenment and growth, the most resounding lesson for me was the reminder of how strong the ego-mind can become when faced with the challenges of life in a body. I found myself far too often trying to figure out how to fix things and impatient with the slow process of recovery. My mind would take me on a "wild river ride" as Eckert Tolle has aptly noted. And I found myself often fighting with it to get it to be still enough to hear Love Itself within.

Meditation became more difficult as my attention struggled to accept the discomfort and stay still long enough to move beyond its incessant noise. It was a true reminder that the very act of living in a body takes a great deal of self-compassion, patience, and acceptance. I was reminded to return to these on a moment-by-moment basis. These three practices are what allowed me to remember that Love Itself is always present and will show me the way if I can have the small willingness to trust and allow.

I am honestly not sure how this following message from Love Itself managed to get through my wild river barriers. It must have been a moment of complete surrender when I finally let my mind be still enough to listen. I have read this message daily ever since and wanted to share it with all of you. There is an additional practice given in the very end that has sustained me and propelled me to a new experience of Love's presence in each moment.

My Child,
Return into the union of our One Mind. Release the belief that there is anything you need to do in this world of form. Release the belief in the self and the illusions of the world of form. Return into the power of our union – only that. There is nothing in the world of form that needs such careful attention. It is not real. Return to what is real – only our union and the power of our united Love and will. That is all. Wear this world loosely, My child. It is not your home. It is not your truth.

Release all your attachments to these illusions of the body. Enjoy and savor the beauty of the world of form, but only so much as it calls you back into unity with our One Love, our One Mind. That is all that needs your attention. Accept the depth of My love for you instead of the small morsels the world will provide. They will always dissipate and return to the dust from which they came. Release your hold, release your clinging to all form. It is fleeting. Only the power of our One Love is real, and thus that is the only truth that prevails. Release your attachment to any outcome as it keeps you from your knowing that you are already home with Me. In every moment, rather see only the Love that permeates and lives and breathes beneath all. For if you could recognize the depth of My love, even in one small flower or tree, then would you never return your awareness

Lesson Nine: You Are Already Home, Complete in Me

to focus only upon the illusions of physical form. Live only in our One Love. For that is all that is real.

Did you notice the practice mentioned? **"For if you could recognize the depth of My love, even in one small flower or tree, then would you never return your awareness to focus only upon the illusions of physical form."** In A Course in Miracles, Workbook Lesson #27 says, "Above all else I want to see." It invites us to repeat this message every 20 to 30 minutes as the repetition will give maximum benefit. I believe it is this depth of love we are being led to see.

As I've been able to return to my morning walks, I notice that it's easier to let my mind be still as I open my heart to consider the love that is beneath just one tree or flower. Shortly after I began this practice, I found myself moved to tears by the love contained within one white dogwood tree. I was quite surprised by the emotion it evoked.

Now, I realize, I pass a million beautiful things in nature almost daily that are emanating with such love, and yet I don't open my heart to consider the depth of love within each. I don't see what is right before me. And more so, I deny myself the power, connection, and union with Love Itself when my heart is not truly open to receive the depth of love within each.

I shared this message with my husband, Jere, again this morning, as we sat on our back deck taking in the beauty of Spring surrounding us. He noted how easy it is to do this when the weather is beautiful, the birds are singing, and the flowers are blooming. "But how do we notice and absorb such love when the sky is gray, the air is cold, and our bodies are aching?" he wondered. I clearly have this struggle myself, and I know we are in good company! But then I realized, how often do we pause to truly see the depth of love given by Love Itself in each individual or even moment within our lives?

There were moments in my recovery from surgery and just before when I could truly absorb and savor the kindness and care in each of my doctors and surgeons. And then there were times when I would look instead with my ego-mind and feel frustrated that none of them could offer me the actual solution to my condition.

In those critical moments, I see how my limited vision kept me from the bigger picture...that all that is real in this world of form is Love. All else is illusion. United with the power of Love Itself, nothing is lacking. I am already home and safe and healed. I want to see only this. I want to see only Love. Above all else, I want to see.

I have since made it my intention to look more closely, with an open heart, to absorb the love that permeates each small moment, tree, creature, and being whose path, I cross. I want to see. And I want to know only the love that I Am within this world of form. May you also see only the Love that permeates and lives and breathes beneath all things. And in doing so, may you come to remember that you are truly, already home with Love Itself.

....

Take 5 to 15 minutes to sit in silent meditation before each *Message of Love*.

Repeating segments of the following may help guide you...

....

Breathe
Just Breathe
Home
Home
Home

Lesson Nine: You Are Already Home, Complete in Me

Message of Love 1: Infinite Possibilities

As you return to Me, in your release of your attachment to the body, the mind, and all your preconceived beliefs, there do you feel the weight of earthly cares and forces lift from your being. There do you find a peace that passes all understanding and an awareness of love that never ends.

As you stay with Me, patient in your trust of what will be revealed to you, does it dawn upon you, a knowing, that you exist in a realm of infinite possibilities each there for your choosing and immediately available upon your acceptance. As you re-emerge with Me in each moment, do you choose again the life you wish and the heaven you wish to see. For it is always and now ever here for you. You need only allow yourself to see and make your choice.

....

**It's fun to ponder the infinite possibilities that are here for me. Here are some possibilities I would like to choose:

*I exist in a realm of infinite possibilities.

....

Message of Love 2:
Always Safe with Me

You are safe here with Me, always safe. Always am I by your side. Always am I one with you here in heaven. Do not try to see with your physical eyes. Rather trust and know it is here.

I am here. Soon will your higher senses awaken to an awareness of that which is always here.

Breathe here with Me. Know and trust. As you look again with trust that home is here, always here, you soon will see. Feel first My love for you. Then feel My love for all of creation. Soon will heaven rise to greet your awakened heart.

....

**Dear Love, I feel your love for me in:

And I feel your love for all of creation as I too feel:

***As I breathe with Love Itself today, I
know, and I trust home is here.**

....

Lesson Nine: You Are Already Home, Complete in Me

Message of Love 3:
Release All Attachments

My child, no longer allow yourself to be bound to the time or space of your life, or your identity in any one place. Return to Me again and again and know with every fiber of your being you are with Me. Always limitless. Always free. Always complete.

Know your home is here and nowhere else. For you are truly complete in Me. Let nothing else complete you. For it is illusion. Let no other time or place confine you. You are truly free with Me, and together we will walk through all time and all spaces and places to all light within all light.

Release all other attachments and let your joy, your truth, your being be always complete in Me. Live in the freedom of our one mind, your natural state with Me.

....

**I'm starting to consider how my attachments to anything but my completion in Love Itself, keep me from realizing my freedom. Here are some attachments I will consider releasing:

*I dwell today in my natural state where I am always limitless and complete. I am one with Love Itself.

....

Message of Love 4:
Your Rightful Place with Me

Come. Come rest with Me awhile. Rest from the cares and worries that weigh heavy on your heart. Come rest. Rest here with Me. Enter My presence. As you breathe in-then out, feel Me here. For I am always here. Sense the doors of your awareness open unto you as you breathe here with Me. And remember, how I remain here steadfast, waiting for you.

Ever patiently, lovingly, waiting for your return.

Come My child, through the doors that open wide for you. Let all else fall away.

Come to Me and find your rest from the weariness of the world of separation. Let the thoughts of fear, of separation and isolation fall off you like a heavy cloak that you no longer need.

And now free, here with Me, do you enter the power of our union, the altar of creation your rightful place with me.

....

**It can be hard to accept the reality that God is truly right here, always as close as my breath. The ego-mind, the voice of separation, always tries to keep me focused away from Love's presence. I will proactively stay attuned to Love's presence by staying intensely aware of my breath and signs of Love's presence such as:

*With each breath I take, I remember Love is right here, within me. As I breathe, I feel my body relax into the peace of this remembering.

....

Lesson Nine: You Are Already Home, Complete in Me

Message of Love 5: My True Being

Welcome home, My child, back into your natural state where the pressures and expectations of your mind fall off you. Can you feel the sweet release of life complete in Me?

The expectations of the world, the separated state, no longer hold power over you. You now remember, you are free. Welcome back into the joy of your true being. Nothing truly has happened, My child. You have simply allowed yourself to reunite with Me, with your awareness of our union.

Your job is only to be and extend the love that you are and celebrate the bliss of your return to love. As soon as you revert to the messages of the ego-mind, the separated state, then do you disconnect yourself from the bliss of our union. You are only love, in that are you in everything and everywhere with Me. In that can you allow yourself to receive and experience all that you desire to immerse yourself within. For in our union is all called forth.

....

**I like to consider that it is my love that is also within every bit of creation. As I look outside my window or sit or walk in nature, I consider my own love extending through: (Name and describe what you experience. For ex: I feel my love emanating and reaching through the pink extending buds of this dogwood tree.)

*My love is extending within and through all I allow myself to experience.

....

Message of Love 6:
Enjoy the Dance

Enjoy the dance that is all this is, a beautiful dance created just for you. Enjoy the rhythm of our steps. We move as one of your accord, quick paced or slow. It matters not. Just enjoy the dance. It is My gift to you.

....

**I want to let myself enjoy this dance with Love Itself! I commit to doing so by:

*Today, I choose to let myself claim joy in this dance!

....

Lesson Nine: You Are Already Home, Complete in Me

Message of Love 7: Nothing Else Exists

Let work give way to knowing. Let effort release to trust. Let worry surrender to love. May all return to peace. For all is complete in Me. Do all with joy that flows of inspiration.

For nothing else exists.

....

**Dear Love, today I acknowledge that all my striving and worries are simply my own resistance to your deep love for me. I surrender my worries about:

In place of these worries, I'm learning to accept:

* Today I place my hand on my heart and breathe in (through my heart) the deep love that is there for me and I breathe out all worry, striving, and doubt.

....

Message of Love 8:
Born of Love

Remember the deep love from which you came. Remember Me and the union we share.

Remember you are born of love and of only love are you created. In your purist, truest essence you are only love. Remember only that. You are of love, created in love, and therefore only love.

Extend only that which you are. All else is illusion, a deception of the ego-mind to keep you separate and blocked off from remembering the love that you are. Breathe here with Me and return to your knowing that all is love, only love, extending love.

....

As I ponder the things and experiences that I love such as:

I can begin to see how my very essence is love because:

***I live each moment of today knowing that my very essence is love.**

....

Lesson Nine: You Are Already Home, Complete in Me

Message of Love 9:
Free Yourself of Judgment

Whatever pain you are perceiving, whether it be emotional or physical, is a misperceived pain. Your thinking mind, the mind that ceaselessly judges and condemns, lays a heavy load upon your being that you have learned to perceive as pain. As you learn to release the self-condemnation, as you forgive yourself your perceived sins, then will all experiences of pain begin to lift from your perception.

Free yourself of judgment and see how your body elevates to the freedom of simply being the light that you are.

....

****As I look at my present perceived pain, I can see that a part of me is judging myself for:

*I acknowledge my self-judgment
today and begin to look with more love,
compassion, and grace for myself.

....

Your Indelible Worth

Message of Love 10:
Float on the Current of My Love

Awaken My child, to the joy of your true being. Bask in this unfolding and new realization of the light that you are and the unbreakable bond that we share. Rest in the bliss as you awaken to life with Me, where all of heaven reveals itself to you. Let each cell awaken to the oxygen that is life in Me. Let each thought rise to the vibration of the song we sing together.

May your vision join with Mine as you see with new eyes, the glistening beauty of creation appearing before you at your beck and call. Float on the current of My love drifting through all the universe. I celebrate this time of your return and joyfully anticipate the song we will sing together.

....

**Love Itself is asking me to rest in the bliss of my awakened life in union with Itself. As I picture myself floating on the current of pure love, I take a moment to sketch out what this would look and feel like. I then add words to describe the current of Love and the oxygen that is life in union with Love Itself. In doing so, I allow myself to begin to see with new eyes.

*Heaven is revealing itself to me today as I look with new eyes.

....

Lesson Nine: You Are Already Home, Complete in Me

MEDITATION

As I awaken today at home with love
I breathe in a soft easy soothing breath
and I feel love expand throughout my being.
I remember,
there is nothing I must do today
but float on the current of your
love for me.
And there I join your angels
in allowing happiness to find completion
in me.
I feel the ease of knowing
I am already home with you,
whole, safe, complete, and free.
It is in this knowing
that I see miracles rise to greet me
as gifts from heaven
reminding me that I am one
with creation,
one with Love
and thus, the creator of my journey,
extending light from heaven
back to earth.
As I awaken today
at home with Love
I remember
I can rest on the current of your love for me.

LESSON TEN:

Release the Illusion of Separation

After the beginning for a split instant
There came a question, "Who am I if I were separate?"
And so, a forgetting was tried, a denial of reality
And a fog came upon the mind that was One
And from the fog came a world of fear
Of isolation, of illusion
In which a moment seemed to last forever
Until a still small voice was heard,
"Remember who you are, remember who
you are, remember who you are."
And then an opening in the fog appeared
To the ear who yearned to listen more
A portal piercing through the fog
Which brought light and music
From beyond the world of form
And angels' notes carried on wings of ecstasy
To a world made drab in fear
And soon the mind who chose to forget
Was lifted through the mist to discover the home, it never left
Sparkling in colors, power, and light.

Lesson Ten: Release the Illusion of Separation

"I am one Self, united with my Creator, at one with every aspect of creation, and limitless in power and in peace."

~ACIM, OrEd.WkBk.95.13

"Feel this one Self in you, and let It shine away all your illusions and your doubts. This is your Self, the Son of God Himself, sinless as Its Creator, with His strength within you and His Love forever yours. You are one Self, and it is given you to feel this Self within you, and to cast all your illusions out of the one Mind that is this Self, the holy truth in you."

~ACIM, OrEd.WkBk.95.18

It was perhaps 17 years ago that I made the decision to commit to taking an hour every morning to read, pray, and journal. I knew if I wanted to find the peace that I craved that I would need to make time to get grounded in that peace each morning. The most vivid feeling memory I have of that time was, simply put, "pure and miserable angst." I recall myself sitting on the couch and deliberately breathing through the chest-pumping anxiety of staying put instead of getting up to do laundry or wash dishes or anything else that would seem to be more significantly productive and valuable.

I realize now that I had bought into others' core messages that to be worthwhile, I should always be producing. At the time, I felt guilty for taking a walk during "work hours" and had a pervasive sense of anxiety most any time I wasn't bringing in the income I thought I should or working an appropriate number of hours. So, it's easy to see that forcing myself to sit through the anxiety was no easy task. I did it nonetheless and allowed the words in my devotionals and *A Course in Miracles* to ease my fear of not being enough. I can't say how long it took for me to finally settle down and enjoy the first 30 minutes of that time. I'm sure anxiety came and went for at least the first six months.

I'm happy to say that my mornings of reading and meditation are now the most blissful part of my day. I confess, however, that the pressure of old toxic messages demanding that I be "working" instead of "being" or even "creating" challenged my ability to even begin writing this book. The following Message of Love came early in the year at the onset of my endeavor to start this book. It was one of the first messages I received and was clearly in response to my own internal struggle. I know I'm not alone, and this Message of Love was meant for me to share with whoever is ready to listen and consider the truth within.

My wish for you is that you will also allow yourself to breathe through the anxiety of staying put and truly take the time to slowly read and absorb the truth in this Message. Notice what you feel in your body. Is there resistance or tension, or do you sense a gradual letting go? Give yourself permission to breathe and reread. Let the meaning soak into your muscles, your bones, and each fiber of your being:

> *When you believe in your heart that you are apart from Me,*
> *When you fear yourself to be alone in a dangerous world,*
> *You cannot but be fearful.*
> *What you have forgotten My beloved child*
> *Is that you are never alone.*
> *I have never left your side,*
> *Nor will I ever.*
> *You fear because you think we are separate,*
> *Working in isolation,*
> *and often against one another.*
> *I reassure you,*
> *That was never the case.*
> *You came from Me.*
> *You are of Me.*
> *We function as one*
> *Or we do not function at all.*

Lesson Ten: Release the Illusion of Separation

Oh, My dear child,
If you only knew,
If you only would allow yourself to remember
The deep love from which you came,
Then would you never feel afraid or lonely or anxious again.
Mine is a love so deep
I formed oceans and mountains and vast color lit skies,
that you might bask in the knowing of My love for you.
But My child you are far too distracted
To allow yourself to accept
these offerings of My love.
Please be still.
Rest in Me.
Wait for Me
I will not fail you.
We are never apart
The whole of creation sings and dances with our
One Expansion.
~Love Itself

Now that you've relaxed into it, contemplate what it means to never be alone. Have you let yourself accept what Love Itself is wanting you to hear? How might that knowledge change how you live in each moment of the day?

Something I figured out from this Message of Love that's changing how I live in each moment is this: If I'm one with God, the Source of all creation, and I can't do anything apart from God, then there's really nothing I need to do on my own. So, I either allow Divine Love to work through me, or I may as well not bother with my own illusions. At the beginning of every counseling session, program, retreat, or talk I give, I've learned that all flows much better as I surrender the outcome to God. I must admit, the times that I forget don't go nearly as well!

There have been times when I've been in very emotional or challenging places in my own life, and I have given the outcome most emphatically to God. Wow! I've been genuinely amazed at times. It has been a true blessing to watch what unfolds in counseling sessions and retreats simply when I get out of the way. There have been countless times when insights and transformative moments have occurred that I never could have planned or orchestrated on my own. I've felt truly blessed as I've gotten to witness such unfolding and realized it was all the power of Love Itself stepping in when I simply stepped back and allowed. I'm also learning to do this in my everyday tasks in life. Rather than trying to power through with to-do lists, I'm learning to connect first with Love Itself and move forward with the next impulse…the action I feel most called to. Sometimes that means just sitting down to rest or call a friend.

One of my most favorite personal times with such an encounter came as I trusted in Love Itself to show up in my first efforts to share the Messages of Love within this book. I had sent a short email to a minister who directs a family camp on the shores of Lake Erie, which I have loved attending from time to time. I simply let him know that I had some inspiring writings I would be happy to share at camp should he need someone to do a prayer or reading. I meant to send a sample or two and, to my dismay, accidentally ended up sending the entirety of my writings! I was shocked and delighted when he responded with an offer to center every evening vesper service around these Messages. And more so, he wondered if I'd mind if he could accompany me with his violin music. What resulted was a more breathtaking and touching experience of Love Itself reaching out to each of us, than I could've ever orchestrated on my own. And all of this resulted from a simple email and willingness to just see how God would show up. Ironically, it was my perceived mistake that opened the door for all of it. In hindsight, I see now there was no accident in any of it.

Lesson Ten: Release the Illusion of Separation

The greatest challenge I've found for myself, however, is learning to step back and get out of the way even when I think I should be able to handle things on my own. It seems far more manageable when I'm already feeling at a loss or like the task is already bigger than me. Somehow, I can give myself permission more easily then. The need to prove ourselves worthy with most of life is so innate, we often don't even realize we're doing it. It's taken me a great deal of patience, and compassionate self-talk to get myself out of the way in writing this book. Over and over, I need to remind myself to step back and let Love show me the way. Are there areas in your own life where you might be trying to prove or earn your worth?

Be patient and kind with yourself as you learn to take this time to be still and listen for Love's voice within you. Even that is an act of surrendering the outcome and getting out of your own way. It's not easy. We are all trying to learn new habits and break old patterns and beliefs that we are alone and therefore should be able to manage alone. Be gentle with yourself and trust this process. Just have a small willingness, and try to let Divine Love do the rest.

....

Take 5 to 15 minutes to sit in silent meditation before each *Message of Love*.

Repeating segments of the following may help guide you...

....

Rest

Just Rest

Rest deeper into Me

Rest a little deeper into Me

Just Rest

a little deeper

Just Rest

Message of Love 1:
Unity with Me

I am calling to all My children to awaken from the dream of separation and join in your rightful place of unity with Me, in the dance of creation. My children may sing many songs to Me, but until you willingly awaken to My song of the true unity that is ours, will the song feel flat and the spirit void of the joy that is My will for you. Awaken, My child, and listen for My voice that calls you home to the dance of creation.

....

**As I listen to the Voice of Divine Love, I begin to hear a more compassionate and encouraging message. It sounds like this (Let yourself write what you feel Love Itself wants you to hear.): My dear beloved child,

*Today I vow to listen to the Voice of Divine Love whenever I'm tempted to instead hear the messages of fear or judgment.

....

Lesson Ten: Release the Illusion of Separation

Message of Love 2: Return Home

Let go the body, and remember Me. Let go the thinking mind and find yourself immersed in Me. Let go the spirit and merge with Me. Release the separation and float with Me. Meet me in the infinite space of nothingness and all that is. Here is your return home with Me, within the deep presence of My love—always here for you, celebrating all you are creating, ever by your side, reveling in each step you take. And always am I empowering you, encouraging you, to know your Truth in Me.

....

**I'm beginning to recognize my truth in God is:

*Today I will try to let my thoughts be still as I sink my awareness into the infinite space of God around me.

....

Message of Love 3: Surrender It Now

The ego-mind counts, compares, measures, judges, and forever will deem you unworthy. It is always in search of something more you must do or fix or accomplish or prove. It is the truest illusion of separation and has been quite successful on its mission. Surrender it now, should you desire your freedom. Surrender it now, should you know your true worth. Surrender it now and will all of creation unlock its mysteries to you, as you return to the knowing of the home you never left.

**Today I'm ready to surrender:

*As I notice the ego-mind in action today, I will pause, take three slow breaths and repeat three times, "I am worthy of peace, and I claim my freedom now."

Lesson Ten: Release the Illusion of Separation

Message of Love 4: Beyond the Ego-Mind

Your ego-mind is in constant search of a problem to be solved, a situation to be resolved, or a person to rescue. It's tireless in its search for fixing or protecting. And yet, that too is merely a defense against your truth, an effort, yet again, to earn your keep or prove your worth. The peace that lies with Me, beyond the ego-mind, is indescribable to your thinking mind. And yet it is fully attainable as you allow yourself permission to lay down all defenses of the ego-mind and simply savor the beauty of life swirling around you. For without the ego-mind, there is only bliss in our unity and celebration of life and love eternally expanding and dancing to the ancient song which plays for all of creation. Come away with Me and see.

....

**As I release the ego-mind, I begin to see:

And I begin to feel:

*Today I commit to savoring the beauty of life swirling around me!

....

Message of Love 5: One Together

When doubt and questioning come, and they will, simply return to your breath in Me. Know again the purpose of the thinking, doubting mind is simply to imply the illusion of separation from Me. But we are not separate. You are not alone. We are one together, and all power, peace, and joy come of your return home to the union that we share. Bask in this knowing. All your needs are met. Creation is yours to share with Me.

....

**As I release the doubting, I begin to see and to accept that all these needs are already being met:

*Today I'm going to try to let go of doubt and trust how Divine Love is taking care of me. I want to give God a chance to show up in a way I never have before.

....

Lesson Ten: Release the Illusion of Separation

Message of Love 6:
Safe with Me

The illusion of separation from Me has been traumatic for you. Out of your perception of isolation have you formed numerous beliefs about your unworthiness for happiness, ease, supply, and love. This sense of isolation, however false, has felt very real to you, and thus you have created your own suffering in ways that are too numerous to count. You may grieve the reality of the pain you have caused to yourself, but only so long as it allows you to release it. Then know that you have been mistaken. You are My child. You are of Me and forever one with Me. I have deemed you worthy, even before your birth into this earthly body. Release your sorrow and receive My comfort now. You were never abandoned, nor were you ever left on your own to figure it out. You just thought you were.

You are home now, safe with Me. And all I have is yours. It's safe to release the protection of fear. You can let down your defenses now. This is truth. You are home. You are safe, whole, loved, and complete in Me.

....

**If I am truly already home and safe and loved, then that means I can begin to let down my defenses and protection such as: (ex: fear, striving, worry, judging...)

*Today I will allow myself to repeat, "I am safe, whole, loved, and complete."

....

Message of Love 7:
Release the Ego-Mind

I have said this before, but it bears repeating; the ego-mind is wholly unnecessary. As you release the illusion of separation, brought on by the ego-mind, then are you free to know the one true answer that fully responds to every question. Release the ego-mind and therein the illusion of separation. Breathe with Me and you will see.

....

**In breathing with you and releasing the ego-mind, I feel:

*Today I breathe in peace, and I exhale all messages of fear and separation.

....

Lesson Ten: Release the Illusion of Separation

Message of Love 8:
I Long to Remind You

My dear child, life in this physical world has confused you so completely. Everything of truth has been turned upside down as you've grown more and more distant from your connection to Me. Turn back to Me. Take time in union with Me, and your eyes will again be opened to see beyond the veil of your illusions. For there is much you have forgotten that I long to remind you. But you are incapable of understanding these truths so long as you stay buried in your to-do lists, shoulds, and endless self-judgments of all you must accomplish. Return to Me, and I will show you your indelible worth, which existed before this earth was formed and will continue into eternity with Me. As you take my hand and walk with Me, you will feel the pressures of this world fall off your shoulders. As your body fades from view and you return to the light that you are, then and only then, will you remember.

    Only joy will you recall as you're lifted to a view of spiraling galaxies and energies of love beyond the physical realm. It is then you will realize the pettiness of your daily worries and seeming efforts to earn your keep in a world that is but only created by you. As you deem yourself worthy to recognize the light that you are and from which you came, then will you know the power that is yours to join Me in a creation of love, made by love. Then will you know and embrace the truth that is you, your indelible worth, in Me.

....

**I'm beginning to remember:

*Today, I most want to remember

_____.
....

Message of Love 9:
One Gift

If I could give you one gift, it would be the ability to stop fixing so that, in its place, you could practice more observing, more being, more savoring, more sinking into each present moment, and therefore more relishing in the sweetness of life.

**Take a walk today and practice receiving this gift. Focus first on five things that you see. Savor slowly and enjoy. Focus next on four sensations that you feel (the wind on your back, the sunshine, etc.) Soak in the bliss of feeling. Third, revel in three sounds that you hear. Next, enjoy two things that you smell. Lastly, savor something that you can taste.

Take your time and allow the mind to be still as you sink into the sweetness of being present with life. Reflect on this experience:

*Today I release the need to fix and will try instead to savor life.

Lesson Ten: Release the Illusion of Separation

Message of Love 10:
Breathe

Rest here with Me a while. Let the song of My birds comfort you. Let your soul take in the colors of My painting for you. Let the steady drip of the rain honor your feelings. Feel yourself surrounded by My love in nature. Feel the breeze on your face and the earth beneath your feet. Know you are fully supported and fully engulfed within the arms of My love for you. Breathe...Breathe...Breathe. I am here. Breathe in My love. Breathe in My peace.

....

**I lift all my feelings to the comfort of Divine Love today:

*I release all expectations of myself today and just breathe.

....

MEDITATION: INFINITE LOVE

Today I trust in a power greater than my own.
Today I trust in Infinite Love
To guide and carry me,
To illuminate my path and open every door
to each dream, desire, and greatest joy.
Today I breathe in the peace of knowing
I am not alone.
Never alone.
Today I trust
My God, My Source, My Inner Guide
Is directing all love, all energy, all power
Through the worthiness that I AM
To co-create with me
The beautiful world I envision.
Today I rest easy and savor the bliss of knowing
Infinite Power, Infinite Wisdom,
Infinite Light, Infinite Love
Walks with me
Every moment of this day!

LESSON ELEVEN:

In Our Union is All Power

Pay careful attention to the symphony playing out before you.
Remember your place in it,
the grand designer
birthed of our union.
~**Love Itself**

"*And now He asks but that you think of Him a while each day that He may speak to you and tell you of His Love, reminding you how great His trust, how limitless His Love. In your name and His own,* **which are the same**, *we practice gladly with this thought today:*

I will step back and let Him lead the way,
For I would walk along the road to Him."
~**ACIM Wkk.155.14,15**

"*If you believe that God created you with a thought or idea, then you can begin to see the power of thought. If you can believe that you created the ego with a thought or an idea, you can see where the power of thought is your power as well as God's.*"
~**ACOL T3:7.2**

"*Nothing that you have refused to accept can be brought into awareness.*"
~**ACIM OrTx:3.64**

Lesson Eleven: In Our Union is All Power

"How do I trust?"

This short and yet challenging question came to me in my Facebook messages shortly before Christmas. It is one to ponder for sure. And there is not necessarily a simple answer. Yet, I love this question and this topic, mainly because the simple willingness to learn to trust opens the door to a wellspring of possibilities. I decided I needed some time to contemplate this deep topic before I jumped into a response. As I sat that morning to meditate, I looked up at my Christmas tree lights, without the aid of my glasses which laid perched beside me. The sweet memories of the Christmas mornings of my childhood flooded back to me as the lights glowed with their soft, yet blurry halos. I remembered the year I got my first pair of glasses and discovered that our tree was bedecked with clear points of lights rather than the blurry auras I had perceived with my limited vision.

I realize that as I've spent more time in meditation and communion with Love Itself over these past few years, my spiritual vision has also grown in clarity. It reminds me of 1 Corinthians 13:12 NRSV which says, "For now we see in a mirror dimly, but then we will see face to face. Now I know only in part; then I will know fully, even as I have been fully known."

Trusting hasn't always come easily for me and given my history with worry, I would say that I was better at listening to the voice of fear rather than the Voice of Love Itself, which is the source of peace and freedom from fear. It seems to me that many of us are looking through blurry glasses when we think of trusting. And often we don't try trusting until we feel backed up against a wall and realize there is no other solution. I can think of the most challenging times of my own life and realize that is where trust…along with surrender, became part of my practice.

You really can't learn trust without first practicing surrender. It wasn't long ago that I thought surrender meant a total letting go. What I didn't realize was that surrender is about letting go of the small-self (ego) beliefs that I must do things alone and that my worth is about being able to make this or that happen. With clearer glasses, I see that surrender to the small self allows you to join with the power of Love Itself as you accept the gift of creating the life you so choose. I'm guessing for most of us that starts with freedom from fear and worry.

Learning to trust in the power of this union comes one small step at a time. My own ability to trust grew exponentially the more I took time in meditation to experience who I am apart from the incessant voice of the ego-mind. Just a moment when the mind lets go, helps you begin to recognize that there is something to you that exists beyond this space and time. It may be incredibly brief at first, but you give yourself the chance to know yourself without the ego operating system. Being the voice that perpetuates the sense of separation from Love Itself, you begin to create space to remember who you are apart from this mechanism. You may experience moments of peace or bliss. You might find yourself crying simply because you finally let down from all the internal pressure and resistance. And soon you may begin to experience impulses or insights that seem to arise within or just following meditation. They may also arise from another experience where your ego-mind has shut down for a while. The more you take small steps to follow these impulses, the more you discover that you are, in fact, being led.

As we take a small step in trust that we are being guided, we begin to look for ways we are being led. And soon we see what we are looking for. If we begin to acknowledge that Love Itself is within us and one with us, wanting us to know our worthiness to join in the co-creative process, then we start to look for signs and indications that support that belief. And we see them! If, however, we focus on our doubt and unworthiness, then the ego-mind creates a veil that keeps us

Lesson Eleven: In Our Union is All Power

from seeing the abundance that is there for us. Instead, we see reasons why we are not supported, because we don't allow ourselves to see beyond the ego's messaging that we are alone and unworthy. Again, we see what we are looking for. And so, we create our own experience.

As the quote above in ACIM says, *"Nothing that you have refused to accept can be brought into awareness."* If we are unwilling to accept that we are one with the power of Love Itself, then we cannot bring that into our awareness. Happily, however, we can begin to accept that we are worthy to join in this united power, and thus allow ourselves to see signs of this truth. It truly takes a small willingness to just take one small step at a time to see what Love Itself would have us see.

So often we get to that place of such surrender, perhaps after a long, hard internal battle, and discover that boundless gifts truly await our willingness to receive them. But then we move on to the next segment of our lives, never really contemplating the amazing blessings that came of surrendering that small-self and trusting in the power of our union with Love Itself. We flip back into denial, thinking that we are isolated and alone again and must go back to doing things with the power of our own feeble little bodies and minds, not even stopping to consider that the power and strength of Love Itself is ready to join us with the fun of creating our own lives no matter what the circumstance.

When I am struggling to let go of my ego-messages of fear, I try to look back to the times when I did step back and trust in the power of my union with Love Itself. Remembering these moments helps me to trust again. As I recall the times when I've surrendered my small-self and let Love lead, I can look with joy at the wonderous ways things played out that were far better than I could've orchestrated with my small ego-self. I usually find that Love Itself has been one step ahead of me all the time and there was never a need for worry!

The following message came to me only a few days before Christmas amid my meditation. It seems, once again, Love Itself was one step ahead of me ready to remind me that we can trust in this gift of creation in union with Love Itself.

This is My gift to you…
That you create the life of your choosing.
You wouldn't give your child a gift
and then tell him he is unworthy or selfish to want to open it.
Allow yourself to receive this gift of My Love, dear child.
Trust in My love and My intent
that you would create this abundant life
of ease and peace, joy, and bliss.
And that you would share the joy of allowing this great gift of My love
with all who are ready to listen.
Yes, tell them how much I love them.
And without reservation or hesitation,
tell them that the gift of creation
of the life of your choosing is
My deepest gift of love to you.
And of course, tell them that I am always here
to share in this boundless adventure with you.
Always loving you and always with you!
~Love Itself

....

Take 5 to 15 minutes to sit in silent meditation before each *Message of Love*.

Repeating segments of the following may help guide you…

....

Breathe
Just Breathe
In Our Union
Is All Power

Lesson Eleven: In Our Union is All Power

Message of Love 1:
Our steps align

There is a knowing that comes with your connection to Me, that is undeniable. It is an unlimited well of power, the power of our united will that we share together. You are learning to sync up with this power, and as you do so you remember, nay, you feel with the entirety of your being the immeasurable love and care I have for you. And you allow yourself to recognize your undeniable worth within creation. It is as a song that calls to you and beckons you to it, to rejoin the dance of creation.

There is much joy and energy in the dance. The more you move with it, the more our steps align, and we flow together as easily as the stars and galaxies align and dance in perfect harmony. Ahh bliss! Ahh joy! Celebration surrounds you as you return to the dance of creation.

**I'm learning to align myself in this dance with creation. Since dancing requires a letting go and attunement with one's partner, I imagine my day as a dance with Love Itself. It would look and feel something like this:

*Today I join the dance of creation as I move and flow with Love Itself!

(To help me attune, I feel my feet on the ground, and I sway gently, in rhythm with Love within me.)

Message of Love 2:
You are Limitless with Me

Always remember there is nothing you need to do of your own accord. Simply unite with Me, and trust in the power of our united will. From this space are worlds created. From this space is your world created. Trust only in the power of our union. Remember, as soon as you venture alone to try to make something happen of your own accord, then do you disconnect from the power of our union. Remember, your trust in Me, your faith, your belief in Me aligns you to join with My power and surrender your own limited power.

Of the body you do nothing. For that is the state of separation. Return to union with Me, in surrender of the body identity, where you elevate yourself to join with My power, with our power of love that has no limits. You are limitless with Me. Live in the grandeur of our union.

Surrender the littleness of the separated state to Me. Return to your natural state of trust, of joy, of ease. My burden is easy. My message is light. You are only light, only love, extending ever outward in union and power with Me. Let go the striving of the separated state.

....

**In union with Love Itself, I accept that I am limitless. I'm learning that I only need to be the love that I am and trust that the deepest desires of my heart are all unfolding beautifully. I envision them and accept that these desires are already coming to pass:

*I am limitless in union with Love Itself!

....

Lesson Eleven: In Our Union is All Power

Message of Love 3:
Look Again from Within

Let go your grasp on the world of form. Release the thinking mind as well. You cling yet to something you know deep within you is not real. You know more than you have allowed yourself to remember. Breathe here with Me. Rest here into Me. This world of form you have created has no power over you. It is truly of your own making. As you let go your grasping and join with Me and see with Me, then does the real world, the world of love illuminate itself for you.

For you are no longer shielding your vision from the truth that is yours. Look again from within, where I am one with you. And let your inheritance reveal itself to you. For nothing is lacking within my Kingdom and you are there now and always.

....

**Dear Love, as I look again from within, I remember:

*I walk in my truth today. Nothing is lacking within me.

....

Message of Love 4: Awaken from Your Sleep

Allow yourself to feel the bliss of our union, and all your heart's desire will reveal itself to you. My Kingdom is unlimited, as are you. Awaken from your sleep, My child. Awaken from your sleep. You are home with Me. I celebrate the return of your knowing.

We together created the world of form. And ye only from the power of our union, of our love, did it arise. As you return to your knowing of our union, do you allow yourself to release the illusion of separation and thus join the power of which we together create.

For truly I say to you, in our union is all power now and forever.

**I've been asleep for too long and my sleeping has created so much unnecessary sadness and struggle. I want to begin telling myself the truth about my union with Love Itself. Here is what I know so far:

*Today I tell myself the truth of my union with Love Itself and thus breathe in the bliss of awakening.

Lesson Eleven: In Our Union is All Power

Message of Love 5:
Feel What You Would Experience

The world of illusion will fall away the more you learn to tune your awareness to My voice. You know the voice of separation is strong. You made it that way. But it is no match for a heart attuned to hear My voice. I would have you know the spirit that you are and the power that you share with Me. For a spirit in complete union with Me is tapped into all My power, the power of creation. This is all you are, and all of which this manifested world is made.

Our unifying power, is all love. All else is a vibration of love manifested by our union.

So, feel what you would experience. Trust in our unifying power and watch the energy of our shared love manifest into any form you choose. Know that you have returned to Me.

Do so knowing it is only the union of our love that is real. All else is a manifestation of our love and therefore, only energy that will shift and move as you so choose in union with My love.

All power is ours.

....

**When I think of what I would like to create with Love Itself, I feel:

(Try writing a story, painting a picture, or creating a vision board to help you feel and savor all that is coming to pass.)

*I savor the joy of all that is coming to pass!

....

Message of Love 6:
You, Complete in Me

The more you let go of the judgment, the fear, the perceived guilt, thus the separated sense of the body, the more you allow yourself to release everything. Then do you join with Me, the energy of pure love, the pure potential from which all springs forth. Release all and join with Me in the unified field of all love. From all love do you lift yourself into the world of our co-creation. For all you create is truly a projection, a creative experience of what you feel within.

This is the power of creation as I allowed it to be and as I called forth, in union with you, our shared will.

You are seeing now, when only love is felt within, then all you envision of that love will rise up in the power of our united love. If you stay restricted by fear or judgment, then do you also project and create a mirror experience of that which is felt within. Thus, is self-forgiveness, release of judgment, and of fear vital to create the life you desire, of which you came here to create.

Know only love. Release all else but love and join me in fulfilling what your soul intended to create and experience, the full expression of you in your natural state of love with Me. Of our united love, of our union, springs forth the greatest joy of creation; **You** complete in Me.

....

**To remember my completion in Love Itself, I realize I need to keep letting go of all judgment, fear, and guilt. Here are some of these defenses against my truth that I am willing to now give to God:

....

*As I look upon myself and others with only love and compassion, I join in the unified field of all love where I am complete and free.

Message of Love 7:
A Disintegration of the Small Self

What you are experiencing is a disintegration of the small self. The matter of the ego-mind, made up of the vibration of separation, is disintegrating as a heavy fog lifting back into sunlight. The illusion of the separated state is falling away bit by bit. And you feel the illusion of the body then dissolve back into the energy of pure love, the merging back into the unified One that is all.

No longer do you function alone and isolated. For you have reunited with the power of our union beyond which there is no other power. From our union comes all of creation. Being only love we call all back to remembering. All in turn will hear the call and draw toward the light that is true that we may all be one.

**I'm learning to let go of my ego-made identity. To do so I let go of what others think of me and of the image and expectations of who I 'should' be such as:

*As I let go of attachments to the small self, I find freedom in simply being me…just love extending.

Lesson Eleven: In Our Union is All Power

Message of Love 8:
The Creative Power of Our Union

See how I make all things new. Creation expands and evolves into the beauty of its truth. What was once barren, and void of life and joy is now overflowing with abundance and energy. The land of milk and honey is before you always. As you align with Me, as you join in the dance of divine union, then does all abundance, all life, all joy rise to greet you and show its beauty that before was hidden from your eyes. See now all as you allow it to become, now that the veil has been lifted and you see with new eyes, the essence of your truth within. Allow your eyes to adjust to recognize the creator that you are and the creative power of our union. See now does our union make all things new as your truth rises to greet you

....

**As I learn to align with Love Itself, I begin to see with new eyes. As I join with Love Itself in this holy instant, I notice:

*I align with Love Itself today and look for abundance, beauty, and joy to show up on my path.

....

Message of Love 9: You Need Do Nothing Alone this Day

Remember, the only thing you truly need to do is return to the awareness of our union.

Return to your knowing that you need do nothing of your own accord this day. For anything sought after or pursued of your separated state will pale to the power of our union. Trust, My child, trust. Let go your littleness, your striving, your fear-based action. Surrender it all to the current of My love for you. And take joy in the witnessing of miracles, the inspiration of My angels in the orchestration of all lined up, ready to open every door for you. Claim only your grandeur and your power in union with Me.

Remember you need do nothing alone this day.

....

**Here are some things I realize I no longer need to do alone:

*I need do nothing alone today!

....

Lesson Eleven: In Our Union is All Power

Message of Love 10:
Your Trust Unlocks the Power of Our Union

Do not fear the grander of our union. Like many others you fear to hope in the grander of our union. For you have trouble trusting in its truth. Yet only in the trust and surrender to our union do you allow yourself to open to receive the benefits of our union. For in your trust do you elevate yourself to the power of our union and thus, the grander that you are and share with Me.

Your trust unlocks the power of our union. Release your fear to hope. For it is true and I will show you. Accept no less than the bliss of our union and all doors will be opened unto you.

....

**I can accept that I may have some fear keeping me from trusting in the power of my union with Love Itself. A part of me is afraid that:

*It is ok to be afraid to trust, but today I want to let Love Itself show me the bliss of our union and the doors that are opening for me.

....

MEDITATION

Home with you
do I remember
I am already complete.
Home with you
do I know
I am worthy of happiness and joy.
Home with you
is there nothing I need to do.
At one with you
do we share all power
to create as we will.
Home with you
is there nothing lacking.
For I remember
I have everything.
I am everything.
And I am ever expanding
into my greatest vision of myself.
At one and
home with you
do I share in the eternity of heaven
with all its splendor and bliss.
Home with you
I am complete.

LESSON TWELVE:

*Your Worth
Is Indelible*

Your worth is indelible
Your worth is unchangeable, irrevocable, undeniable
Forever imprinted in eternity
It is
Beyond measure
Unalterable
Inevitable
Irreversible
Unerasable
Your worth
Is now
And eternally
Sealed within the love of *Love Itself*
It is
Outside time and space
Independent of any bodily condition
Unabraded by status or money
Skill or talent, success, or failure
Your worth is
Decidedly carved
In the heart of The Divine
And so, it is as it was created
Indelible

Lesson Twelve: Your Worth Is Indelible

"Your worth is beyond perception because it is beyond doubt. Do not perceive yourself in different lights. Know yourself in the One Light where the miracle that is you is perfectly clear."
~ACIM, OrEd.Tx.3.60

"Like you my faith and my belief are centered on what I treasure. The difference is that I love only what God loves with me, and because of this, I treasure you beyond the value that you set on yourselves, even unto the worth that God has placed upon you."
~ACIM, OrEdTx:13.33

"It is a choice to know yourself as you always have, or a choice to know your Self as God created you."
~ACOL—Book One, The Prelude C:P.18

After a long walk, mixed with tears and contemplation, rumination, and self-doubt, I returned home to the sweet surrender of shade under my maple tree. I sat and breathed as I let go of months of inner tension. A stillness surrounded me that blessed me with release from my endless thinking and questioning. It was a sad and painful time to have my marriage and life seem to collapse around me. I doubted every fiber of my being. And yet, through the stillness, I heard a soft Voice whisper, "Remember who you are, remember who you are." Someone was speaking to me, and it didn't seem to be me. And who was I? I really wasn't sure anymore. I tucked the message away as if it was a note from my mother, I didn't quite understand but thought I should probably hold onto it just in case the meaning occurred to me. I realize now, looking back, that was one of my first encounters with Divine Love reaching through to speak to me.

Let's move quickly through the endless days of tears, struggle, and hibernation, to the point where I decided perhaps, I could begin living again. And by living, I mean, considering I could date again. This, in fact, turned into a roller coaster ride of on-line dating experiences. I oscillated between addictive infatuation, to the huge let down of the actual date, in which neither of us proved to be what we hoped, expected, nor idealized in our minds. I noted to myself that clearly, the right man for me did not live in my city, my state, or any neighboring state. I decided any man of good character was probably not good looking, so I crossed all good-looking men off my list. It was becoming a small list of possibilities. From my place of lack, unworthiness, and doubt, I created only limitations. I had no idea that my own mental state was creating my actual experience.

Thankfully, I eventually recalled the concepts of the Law of Attraction. This helped me become wise enough to realize I needed to be more precise about *what* exactly I hoped for in my next relationship. I remembered that I needed to consider that just maybe, I was worthy to receive that. I wrote out a vision of who that sweet love would one day be and then within a matter of a few months became quite frustrated when God did not allow him to cross my path. And so, in exasperation, I threw up my hands and yelled to the heavens, "I Give! I surrender! I'm done trying so hard to make this happen. Clearly, it's not working. Whenever you think it is the right time, God, I'll be ready!" And so, I did. I truly surrendered. I got off the internet. I let go of the addictive searching and started to focus on caring for myself. I took more walks, joined a gym, and tried daily to remind myself to trust and surrender.

As I look back now, I see that the surrender and giving the outcome to God came easier simply because I felt I had no choice. Everything I had tried wasn't working anyway. The trusting part was more difficult. Absorbing the concepts within **A Course in Miracles** gave me the peace and sense of worthiness I so craved. I read a little each morning as it became a lifeline of hope and safety

Lesson Twelve: Your Worth Is Indelible

that sustained me. The messages within gave me the help I needed to trust amid surrender.

And then he appeared. I noticed him across the gym, lost in his music and his weightlifting routine. For a while, I just noticed. And then I saw he was there every Thursday at 7 pm. Coincidently, so was I. We started with a few friendly hellos, and then I came up with some reason to ask him for advice. And then, well, the rest feels nothing less than miraculous. He turned out to be everything on my vision list multiplied by 10 in most cases. I could not have created in my own mind a man more utterly right for me. I've learned that when you put your requests up to Love Itself, all your desires are considered together in creating the highest version of all you've intended. That was the case when it came to the angel that seemed to drop into my life.

I had hoped for a partner who could share in my love of nature and flowers. As it turned out, Jere not only loves and nurtures nature down to the very last bee, he loves planting and nurturing flowers, trees, and birds. And the biggest gift Love Itself coordinated is a partner who also nurtures me. Nearly the entire first two years of our relationship, he found some way, either a note or a message on my voicemail, to tell me I was more than enough just the way I am. When I was struggling with all I could not control around me, he would lock eyes with me and help me repeat the serenity prayer. He helped me heal. He helped me remember who I am.

Looking back now, I can see the elements that had to come together: the vision/request, the surrender, the trust. Most importantly, I needed to realize I was worthy of my heart's desire *and trust* that Divine Love wants that for me as well.

It's been 18 years since Divine Love responded wholeheartedly to my surrender, trust, and willingness to believe in my own worthiness. Yesterday morning, my meditation yielded what I can only explain as an awakening that answered that original call, "Remember who you are." The writing that follows flowed from this experience:

Remembering

In the silent spaces deep within
When all the pushing and pulling lets go
And I find myself sinking into being—into breath
When thoughts release
And all the attachment to this body
Unlocks
When all around I hear only birds
And gradually even their songs grow distant
Then there appears
An opening
And within
An angel
And the sweetest fragrance
And a knowing
Here am I
One with All Source
Love Itself Am I
Remembering Who I Am

I'm realizing, more clearly now than ever, that I was looking for my own worthiness in all the wrong places. In looking for it outside of myself, I see that my sense of peace and worth was always dependent on some external factor. It kept me feeling like a victim to whatever another person thought, or whatever life situation was happening around me. I had to dig deep enough to first consider that I am, in fact, more than I ever allowed myself to believe. I had to let myself start to let go of the old messages I told myself and consider that maybe I am part of something Divine. Perhaps there is a greater part

Lesson Twelve: Your Worth Is Indelible

of me from which I've disconnected. I even found myself grieving the loss of feeling that separation from Divine Love for so long.

I had to let myself start to reach for that connection again and the truth Love Itself wanted to reveal to me about my worth, about who I really am. I had to be willing. I had to be open. I had to be vulnerable and raw and bring my most profound doubts about myself to that greater part of me...to Divine Love. And I had to be willing to listen for the compassionate, loving response that was there all along. That loving response is there for you too. It's within you, and it's within the Messages of this journal. Give yourself permission to be even a little more open, a little more willing to consider Divine Love is trying to reach you, right now. Love Itself wants you to remember.

Take 5 to 15 minutes to sit in silent meditation before each *Message of Love*.

Repeating segments of the following may help guide you...

Breathe
Just Breathe
Love
Love
Love

Message of Love 1:
Perfect As You Are

Be easy on yourself. You are so quickly ready to condemn and judge yourself. You have spent too long training yourself to look for ways you are unworthy. There would be no need for forgiveness in your world if you could only learn to forgive yourself. Forgive yourself of all your perceived shortcomings and limitations. As you create these beliefs in your mind, then do you keep yourself from knowing the radiant light that you are. You, therefore, halt my love and power from extending through you. Be easy on yourself, I say. Try to love yourself as I love you, never perceiving a flaw or shortcoming. You are my beloved child, immensely loved, perfect as you are. Release yourself only to My love, and know the light that you are.

....

**Today I'm going to forgive myself for any and all my perceived shortcomings. I forgive myself for:

I also forgive myself for that which I cannot fix or control:

*I pledge to be more compassionate, loving, and forgiving of myself today.

....

Lesson Twelve: Your Worth Is Indelible

Message of Love 2:
You Are My Guiltless Child

I would speak to you today of the sins your separated mind has caused you to believe in and therefore hold as a hammer over your own head. You are continually suppressing your light as you fear you are unworthy and guilty. Believe me, My child, when I tell you, you cannot sin against me. My will is love, and only that is, therefore, possible. When you believe you have sinned, you have misled yourself into thinking it is possible to act separately from me. We are One, and that is all. Only love can come from our union. All else is an illusion. You are my guiltless child, forever loved, forever Mine, ever in My heart. I sent My son to you to teach you only that. My will for you is love. His dying on the cross only proved that there is nothing you can do to keep Me from loving you. No illusion of your mind, even of the pain caused to Him, could ever separate you from My love. Love is what I Am. Love is what you are. Forgive yourself your imagined sins. You are my guiltless child.

I love you so.

....

**I'm ready to consider I am a guiltless child of God. Knowing I am guiltless frees me to live my life from a whole new perspective. As a guiltless child of Divine Love, I no longer need to worry about:

and I am free to:

*Today I consider that I am a guiltless child of Divine Love.

....

Message of Love 3: Forgive Yourself

There is an opening that comes within the space in which you release your hold on self-judgment, criticism, and guilt. Often you disregard this internal resistance to the truth that is you. You fail to realize how great is your need to forgive yourself for all your perceived transgressions. For the lock of self-judgment bars you from the truth that is you and from realizing the grandeur that is you. Such criticism blocks the passageway of your joining to My power, My love, and our connection, which is the completion that is you.

Be still a while. Search your heart for the places where you are called to let forgiveness in. Open your heart to this gift, which only you would withhold from yourself. Soon you will feel the release and opening to the joy of angels and Me celebrating our reunion; a reunion back to your truth, a reunion of remembering all the joy, all the love that is you.

Forgive yourself and join Me in the opening where our lights will merge again as one, and you remember the truth, joy, and beauty that is you.

....

**Write a loving forgiveness letter to yourself in three parts.

Dear me,

I'm sorry for the pain I've caused you by being so harsh and critical of you in the following ways: I'm also sorry for:

I forgive you for:

Thank you for:

....

Lesson Twelve: Your Worth Is Indelible

*Today I will pay attention and notice where I am judging myself. I honor my pain by saying, "I'm sorry and I forgive you." I then breathe with Love Itself and listen for Love's compassionate response.

Message of Love 4:
Time to Claim

Do you yet know you are worthy?
Have you felt the bliss of connecting with My power,
your one true source?
It is time for you to live your life in the fullness of your knowing.
Now is it time to be fully that which you are.
Throw off the old habits that no longer serve you.
Step out of the old wineskins and into the blessed new life
to which I've been calling you.
Be that which you came to be.
Nothing less will suffice you any longer.
You are the child of a King.
And everything I have is yours.
It's time to claim it all.
First your worthiness,
then the truth of who you are as My child,
Now the right to enjoy, celebrate, and live,
in the fullness of all our family gifts,
creating together
this life of
ever-expanding, evolving love, and beauty.

....

**Recognizing my innate, indelible worth, helps me to begin to see that I Am One with My Creator. Therefore, my innate passions, desires, and longings

Lesson Twelve: Your Worth Is Indelible

are part of our shared will. The deepest longings of my soul are Source extending through me. I'm learning that my passions are an extension of Love Itself expressing in me. It's time to celebrate and support my passions! I can start doing this by:

*Today I give myself full permission to daydream about my passions, trusting they are an extension of Divine Love expressing through me!

Message of Love 5:
Never-Ending Supply

Now must you learn to live in constant connection to Me, the Source of all knowing and the Source of freedom from all limitations. For I am always speaking to you, and there is no point where I am unavailable. As you desire to extend My love, must you first be always open to receive My love. And therefore, know the worthy being that you are. To be the physical expression of My love, stay close to Me, always aware of My breath and life in you. For then may you always draw from the well of My never-ending supply of peace, of healing, of nourishment both in the physical realm and always your connection to the spiritual realm.

....

**Dear Love, when I allow myself to sit and feel my connection to you, I feel:

*Today, I commit to pausing and waiting to feel my connection to Love Itself.

....

Lesson Twelve: Your Worth Is Indelible

Message of Love 6:
Your Space of Truth

Do you understand that when you doubt yourself, you question Me? For we are intricately woven, and there is no point at which you end, and I begin. We are one, and thus, you must learn to trust yourself as you are learning to trust Me. I am here in your greatest desire, your deepest longing, the space where you are your most authentic self. I am your space of truth, your most profound knowing, your greatest peace.

As you learn to allow yourself to live and be, here in Me, in your space of truth, then will you come to see, there is nothing beyond your ability to know and experience as perfection. You will learn to trust all of life exactly as it is. And you will learn to trust your own unfolding and evolving precisely as it is. Essentially, you will learn to trust life and your ability to live and breathe as the flow of it all. For that is truly, your space of truth.

No more need you to worry, "Am I good enough here or worthy in that?" Now may you simply be, as life itself, as love itself, expressing through itself. Now is there nothing you need to do, and there is nothing you must do. Simply know you are free to live in your natural state; aligned with pure acceptance of all that is, and joyful in the knowing, you are free to create as you wish.

Now is life as you choose to see and perceive, in happy anticipation of the wondrous delights awaiting you.

....

**Dear Love, I see now how much doubting of myself limits your ability to work and extend Your power through me. I'd like to take this time to name and release my doubt into your

compassionate care and love. In the space below, draw a symbol of Divine love for you and within it write, "I give you my self-doubt about:" (Name the doubt you need/want to surrender.)

**Now lovingly hold that visual of your self-doubt in your hands and release it up and out to your Higher Power. In exchange for releasing your own self-doubt, you can then allow your hands to receive the Power of Divine Love to move in place of your perceived shortcomings. Trust that as you surrender your shortcomings to your Source, you allow a far higher Power of Divine Love to move and work through you. Breathe out as you release your shortcomings and breathe in as you allow Divine Love to return in their place. Breathe in and breathe out in this happy exchange.

*I am Love Itself, expressing through itself.

Lesson Twelve: Your Worth Is Indelible

Message of Love 7:
My Deep Love for You

My child, you create much unnecessary suffering and sadness for yourself when you doubt your worthiness to receive the happiness that is My will for you. My angels surround you day and night, and their only mission is to make your path clear and light for you. You, however, block your ability to receive their aid and assistance when you deem yourself unworthy by your very thoughts of self-judgment and your focus on what is lacking.

Sit with Me, My child, if only for a moment, and consider My deep love for you. Consider all that might be, nay, is already, waiting for you should you only consider how worthy I deem you to receive all of it. My greatest joy for you is your pure and truest happiness. Trust that it is prepared for you. Look for it on the path My angels lay before you. Allow yourself to receive all the gifts of My kingdom. For I want nothing less for you. Why should you refuse it? Dare to dream it possible and it will be so.

....

**As I shift my focus to acknowledge how much God loves me and wants only happiness for me, I can begin to notice where God has been showing me such love and support. I now can see God's love, support, and desire for my happiness showing up in the following ways:

**I commit to looking for more of this as I acknowledge that my focus and intention create what I see.

....

Message of Love 8:
Being and Becoming

The only thing that tires you in the process of creating is in forgetting that your worth is indelible, forever sealed within the truth of our union. You weaken when you mistakenly allow your worth to attach to the outcome of any of your creations. So much internal effort and pressure weighs on you and steals your energy. Remember this, My joy is in watching you enjoy this journey of discovery and becoming. Never do I judge your ability to produce or create. Always, I revel only in your joy of being and becoming. Just as you take joy and revel happily in the witnessing of a child learning to walk or your puppy learning a new skill, so do I celebrate you. Enjoy the being and becoming. Attach your worth, not to any outcome.

....

** Whenever I feel upset or distressed, I may look within and see that I have attached my sense of worth to some outcome or situation. My Source is telling me that I no longer need to do this! I now acknowledge, I often attach my worth to these situations or outcomes:

*I am as Love created me. My indelible worth is dependent upon nothing.

....

Lesson Twelve: Your Worth Is Indelible

Message of Love 9:
Complete in Me

Create without attachment. For attachment leaves you caged, and you are not meant to be caged. You are created to fly free in the story of your own creation. Yet the moment you forget who you are and whose you are is the moment, you entrap yourself and believe your worth is now attached to that which you create. Take heed as you strengthen your wings and learn to fly. Tether yourself not to any of your creations. For they are simply props in the unfolding story of you becoming you—fully you—complete in Me, and one with all that is.

> **My worth is attached to nothing. I am worthy and more than enough just the way that I am. Knowing I am free of all attachments, I see myself flying free and joyfully creating:
>
> *Today I am free to create without attaching my worth to any of it.

Message of Love 10: Wait for My Impulse

There is much you believe you must do; I know. If you tune closely to the sensation within you, you will notice the pressure of your mind, beckoning you to earn your worth by your efforts to be productive. I caution you not to let this be your guide. Stay with Me, attuned to My presence and power within you. Wait here with Me until all pressure ceases, and there arises within you joy and excitement at what you would like to do with Me. Wait for My impulse within you, accompanied by a joyful yearning within your soul, and you then will know the path to follow. Now savor the journey with Me.

....

**Today, I'm going to focus on feeling good and just being. I will let myself be inspired to action instead of forcing action because of a need to earn my worth. As I breathe and release the pressure to produce (releasing all judgment) I notice that I am feeling an impulse to:

*Today, I trust my impulse and what feels right for me! If I'm feeling pressured, overwhelmed, or heavy, I will stop and breathe and wait for efforts and measures of my worth to subside. I'm learning that I am more than enough just as I am. I let Divine Love guide me this day.

....

Lesson Twelve: Your Worth Is Indelible

MEDITATION

Remember the light that is you,
Far beyond which there is no other.
You are brilliant and true, ever extending outward.
Remember the spark that is within,
Joyful, free, full of wonder, play, and imagination.
You shone brightly even before
This physical world existed, and you will
Continue to shine after all things physical are no more.
Remember the truth, that is you.
Worthy beyond measure
Immensely loved, divinely crafted,
Ever belonging to
All The Love That Is.
Remember the truth, that is you.
Remember who you are,
Apart from any earthly thing or accomplishment.
You are a child of Divine Love.
You are Divine Light,
Whole, free, and limitless.
Remember My dear child,
You are mine.
I Am Yours.
We are never apart.
For that, you can be sure.
Remember the Light that is You!
Just remember.

❋ ❋ ❋

Exercises for Emotional Clearing and Absorbing Truth

#1

A Daily Practice in Blissful Trust

You have spent so much of your life thinking you must rely on your own efforts.

Learning to trust you are connected to a power far greater than your own, who loves you and knows your worthiness to receive, is an exercise in unlearning all you have trained yourself. This will take time, practice, and diligence. Yet as you begin to practice, you will discover this way of living is far easier, more natural, and considerably lighter than you could ever imagine.

As you begin each day, perhaps before you get out of bed, you can awaken to trust in your worthiness to align with and receive the Power of Divine Love. (Remember the significance of repetition in forming new neural pathways and instilling new belief systems.)

STEP 1) BE OPEN TO LOVE'S PRESENCE WITHIN YOU.

Put your hand on your heart space and allow yourself to feel and accept God's deep love for you. It might come as a feeling of gratitude as you acknowledge moments in nature or with loved ones where you have felt the presence of Love as a gift to you. You might say to yourself, **"Today, I trust that a power greater than this body loves me and is working through me and for me. I will be ever** mindful to pause when my first impulse to act or worry arrives. I will align my awareness with this Power, my loving guide. I will wait and remember I can put full trust in Divine Love to be already at work in all things that are important to me today."

STEP 2) IDENTIFY THE DESIRE OF YOUR HEART.

Name specifically what it is for which your soul longs, and note that you are open to accepting that this is what Love Itself wills for you as well. Be willing to accept this gift of love.

STEP 3) NOTICE RESISTANCE.

Stop and note within your body any resistance to allowing this Higher Power to flow within you and take care of things for you. This resistance might present as fear, worry, or any sense there is something you are responsible for fixing. It may also feel like a pressure in your chest, uneasiness in your stomach, anxiety, or another physical discomfort. Remember, there is nothing you must fix. Allow yourself to breathe love into those spaces that feel resistance. Feel them soften as you breathe and repeat, "I trust you (Love Itself/my Higher Power) are already on this and working everything out for me. I believe in my worthiness to receive this gift of love. I will rest in the ease of knowing it's already taken care of."

STEP 4) SURRENDER THE OUTCOME.

Surrender the outcome of this, along with the means, to the power of your union with Love Itself. You don't have to do anything or know how it will happen. Just give it to God to work out, trusting in the power of your union. Place your hand on your heart and take three slow deep breaths (in union with Love Itself) and acknowledge your gratitude that Love's got this, whenever you start to doubt or worry.

STEP 5) FOLLOW INSPIRATION.

If you feel inspired or led to action, follow the inspiration as you trust in divine guidance.

STEP 6) SAVOR THE ABUNDANCE AROUND YOU.

Focus on what feels good and what is going well. Name all for which you are grateful and all the ways God is always providing and taking care of you. Notice the abundance, the love, the support, the mystery of life around you and in all of nature. Let yourself *feel and savor* the abundance as you feel its ease within your body as opposed to simply naming and thinking about it.

See how your trust grows with each small step of surrender!

"I trust in the Divine unfolding of my heart's deepest desires."

#2

Clearing Blocks with The Tree of Judgment

As I mentioned early, often, we need to do some emotional work to clear the brush of heavy emotions so that we can be in a more transparent space to allow loving messages to flow in. The following exercise can be used at any time you are feeling heavy and unable to release the weight/emotional blocks using meditation alone. You will need to pull out a sheet of plain paper and draw whatever form of a tree you would like upon it. Be sure that the tree includes open branches, a spacious trunk, and open roots, all upon which you may write. Feel free to color it any way you wish after you have completed the exercise!

When we are feeling down, heavy, stuck, or just plain unhappy many of us can stay there endlessly without knowing what to do or how to move out of this state. Training ourselves to acknowledge, honor, and understand these feelings will allow us to move through and beyond them with greater ease, less suffering, and more quickly than otherwise. It will also help us to be more open to receive and absorb the Messages of Divine Love. The Tree of Judgment is an exercise that can help you do just that when followed up with the Tree of Compassion.

In working the Tree of Judgment, we start by sitting still for a few moments and just breathing. We give ourselves permission to tune into our bodies by simply taking time to just breathe in and out and beginning to move our awareness into our body. It's a bit like focusing the lens of a camera. The more you breathe in then out... slowly, and just focus into your body, you begin to notice physical sensations. Scan your sensations in your body from your head down to your toes. While this is the Tree of Judgment, there's no need to judge what you are feeling right now! Just notice! Is there a heavy feeling in your chest? Do you notice tension in your shoulders? Is your jaw clenched? Physical discomfort is often the first clue to help you look further to recognize the accompanying emotions. As you start to identify what you are feeling physically, then you can begin to ask yourself what emotions are there as well. Again, don't judge. Just notice. Then start at the top of the tree and begin to write down all unpleasant emotions you notice as they resonate with the physical sensations. For example, if I feel a pressure in my chest and begin to sit with it, I might then recognize that I'm feeling overwhelmed or sad. Write everything that comes to you without censoring any of it. Place all these feelings and sensations on the branches at the top of the tree. Allow yourself to lean into these feelings without judgment. Let them move through you. If you feel like crying do so.

After thoroughly writing all your unpleasant feelings on the branches, then move down the tree to the trunk. Along the trunk of the tree, write down the negative messages and expectations, you have been telling yourself, that have been leading to unpleasant feelings. Following some of the sad feelings, I might discover underlying messages I'm telling myself like; "you'll never feel better, this isn't going away, this is your fault, you can't handle this, you're just weak, you just need to push through, you should be better than this, you shouldn't feel this way."

In the final step, you move down to the roots of the tree where you will identify the primary toxic/negative core belief at the source of all of it. We often use the word toxic because we acknowledge how poisonous the entire message is to our emotional, mental, and physical wellbeing. For most, this message is rooted in some form of self-judgment, internal shame, or sense that your worth is dependent upon an outcome i.e.: I'm not enough, I'm worthless, I'm unlovable, I'm insignificant, etc. It might come in the form of should i.e.: "I should be able to fix things on my own or I'm responsible for others' happiness," etc. These are just a few examples. In the case I've used of sadness, the core message might be, "If I were enough, I wouldn't be feeling this way." If you are struggling to identify your toxic core message, you may want to talk with a trusted and healthy friend or family member or therapist.

Next, proceed to The Tree of Compassion where you can begin to shift your negative belief system.

#3

Absorbing Love with the Tree of Compassion

Compassion is always here waiting for you. Are you allowing yourself to be in the place to receive it? You are coming to understand the deep love your Divine Source has for you. Now you must allow yourself to integrate the truth and reality of that Love into each moment of your life. In the Tree of Compassion, you will enable yourself to contemplate the depth of such deep love more fully for you as you are coming to understand it. You then allow yourself to absorb the truth of it into your being and begin to see how this shapes and creates your life experience. You may use this tree exercise in one of two ways:

1. As a follow-up to the Tree of Judgment when you are feeling heavy or down or stuck in some way and/or when you recognize this heavy feeling is blocking you from absorbing the truth within each Message of Love.

2. As a follow-up to each Message of Love, and you want to absorb this truth more fully into your being and therefore into your life experience.

✳ ✳ ✳

Exercises for Emotional Clearing and Absorbing Truth

AS A FOLLOW-UP TO THE TREE OF JUDGMENT:

In the Tree of Judgment, you recall that you will work from the sad feelings within the leaves (at the top of the tree) down the trunk to finish with the Negative/Toxic Core Message at the roots of the tree. You will then begin the Tree of Compassion at the same place where you left off, the roots. You'll now need to draw a second tree. Here you rewrite the Negative Core Message into the compassionate truth you realize that Love Itself would say (or that you wish you could hear) to you instead. In the example used above, you might rewrite your negative message to say, "I am as God created me. I am more than enough just the way I am." **Write this new message upon the roots of your new tree.**

From this new loving and compassionate core message, you will then be able to work your way up to the trunk where you will write more loving, encouraging statements you can then tell yourself because of this new core message. With the new core message written above, one could then say, "All my feelings are okay. This will pass. It's okay to feel sad about this. I can be kind and caring to myself."

By the time you get to the branches, you will notice that your feelings are lighter, easier, and more hopeful because of this Truth, you are allowing yourself to receive instead. Write the new, lighter feelings on the branches.

Breathe easy and take your time with this exercise. Allow yourself to let your new message flow into and through your being as it would flow through the energy of the roots and up through the trunk into the life of the branches. Notice how this reshapes your entire outlook, energy, and perspective. ***For it is true, we see and experience without what we have first seen and experienced within.***

*If you could take the time to do this exercise anytime you are feeling down or heavy-hearted it would not be too often.

❋ ❋ ❋

AS FOLLOW UP TO READING A MESSAGE OF LOVE:

The Tree of Compassion can here be used to help you more fully absorb and integrate each Message of Love into your being and life experience. Read slowly through any Message of Love within this book. It doesn't matter which. I recommend you take the time to do this exercise following the reading of each Message of Love if you are willing and able to make the time. Allow yourself to sit and breathe and release all resistance for 5 to 20 minutes before each reading. Say to yourself that you are open to receive this Message of Love as it is directly from your Creator and meant for you. If you are willing and open to considering that Divine Love wants to speak directly to you, then you will recognize and feel the Message you receive will be specifically for you. There may be one million people reading this Message, but each one will accept it as it is meant specifically for them.

Love Itself wants you to know, *"My Love and My Truth flow through these Messages and are always flowing directly to you. I am ever ready to speak with you and come to you in any way you allow. If you allow yourself to receive Me in each Message as you read, then your experience of Me and My love for you will be specifically for you. I am here now. I am here in this reading. Allow yourself to accept this. Feel Me. RECEIVE ME. Take in this Message, which is meant just for you. After you have done so, sit and breathe. Let it soak into you. Feel whatever feeling comes."*

Then begin the exercise at the roots of the Tree of Compassion. Write the Main Core Message you personally received from the reading, upon the roots of the tree. Then work your way through the trunk writing whatever positive, encouraging thoughts and statements now are flowing because of this Truth, this new Core

Message. When the trunk is full, you then can begin to write the feelings that result upon the branches and leaves.

Feel free to color and play as you fully absorb and relish in the joyful news of this Truth you are fully realizing. Add any words, thoughts, colors, or pictures as you soak in this new way of looking at yourself and the world. ***For it is true, whatever you first see within, will give you the eyes to create and see the world around you.***

#4

Integrating Your Truth

Your life has shown you some or perhaps many experiences that have confirmed a knowing deep within you that Love Itself is present and acting in ways you can and cannot see. Often, you enjoy them for a moment but don't fully allow yourself to accept and integrate the truth which has just revealed itself to you. Instead, your ego-messaging may lead you to doubt, disregard, or minimize the full depth and reality of your experience. The voice of separation is set up to discredit any experience of truth revealed to you. Thus, you continue to maintain the old patterns of belief that life must be hard, that there must be suffering, and you are alone and unsupported. You must allow yourself to go back and integrate these truths you've disregarded along the way. Feel the depth of them. Fully bring them together into your awareness so that you can accept the full reality that has been revealed to you along the way.

Allow yourself to draw a large heart or personalized symbol depicting the totality of you. Within and around your symbol, write and describe your experiences or awareness of a higher knowing. Perhaps it was a moment by the ocean or watching a sunset or a child. Maybe it was in meditation or revealed to you in a moment of synchronicity with nature or a loved one. You may also have heard a voice of love or guidance speak to you that you felt deeply was not your own. Record also the times that Love Itself has opened doors or guided you along a path to greater clarity or insight. Name the times you gave a request up to Love Itself, surrendered and trusted, and then it came to pass. The insights and remembering will come as you allow. If you cannot yet remember, allow yourself a simple willingness to notice and record these experiences as they are revealed to you.

After you have listed what you can remember, even if it's just one moment, allow yourself to write or draw in detail the specifics of the moment. Identify the circumstances, color, sounds, shapes, images, and feelings that arose. Give one word or phrase to summarize the core truth of the experience. Allow yourself to revel and bask in the feeling memory of it.

When the feeling memory is very real to you, and you have the felt sense of knowing within you, take some time to do the following breathing exercise to help integrate it within your body: Utilizing your index and middle fingers as a guide to facilitate the breathing between your left and right nostrils of your nose, follow this pattern for 3 to 5 times. Breathe in slowly through the right nostril and breathe out through the left. Then breathe in through the left and out through the right. Continue in this pattern breathing in again through the nostril in which you just exhaled. Allow yourself to relax into the felt sense of the memory as you breathe.

Take time daily to call up this feeling memory of knowing by utilizing this breathing exercise and naming the core truth revealed. If ever you are feeling anxious, fearful, or doubting, remember to tell yourself the truth as you now know it. Repeat the above breathing exercise and bring the feeling memory of this truth into your present moment.

#5

Soaking into your Natural State with Love Itself (in italics)

You have great difficulty allowing yourself to live in your natural state of joy and simple trust in My Love and Power to guide you through your day. Most often, there is internal resistance to allowing life, including yourself, to be as it is. You have trained yourself to disregard your natural state and, in exchange, tried to make something more worthy of yourself. Essentially, you are saying, "I am not worthy as I am, and therefore, I must recreate myself into something more worthy." Thus, there is an intense internal pressure that you have carried for so long that you mostly don't even recognize exists.

It's time to start acknowledging this pressure, this effort to recreate yourself so that you can live in your natural state more easily.

Start first by soaking your awareness deep into every fiber of your being. Start with the top of your head, and move your way down very slowly through each body part. Feel deeply into each cell, each fiber, each muscle, and allow it all to simply be as it is. Remind yourself there is nothing you need to fix or change or do. Just feel, with loving compassion, from deep within and allow it all to be what it is. Notice physical sensations, notice emotions, notice your breath, and allow it all to just be as it is. Notice how the sensations rise and fall like a tide in the ocean rises to the edge of the shore, cascades down, and then recedes back again. Learn to ride the wave with ease and acceptance. Feel the inhale of your breath move into each space with love and compassion. Feel the release and open acceptance with each exhale. Notice how all of it softens and releases with simple allowing and acceptance.

Now, from this state, you are practicing the acknowledgment that there is nothing you must do and nothing you must fix. You are allowing yourself to be in your natural state, with pure acceptance and no judgment. It is from this state of being that you learn to let yourself be in each moment. If, from this natural state of grace, you feel inclined to take a nap or take a walk, or make something soothing for yourself, then do so. If you feel inspired to work on something, then do so. There is nothing you must do as you acknowledge you are worthy as you are. *There is nothing you must do as you recognize you have aligned with Me (Divine Love/God/Your Source), who will guide and inspire you in each step you take. So, wait to see what you **feel** like doing. Wait for inspiration to act. Let what feels most natural and easy guide you. Trust that from this place of your natural state, where you are allowing Me to guide you, you will not fail. For you have aligned with the Power of Divine Love, and I will not fail you.*

#6

Absorbing Gratitude

To increase your awareness of the power of focus, first focus your attention on something that worries you. How does your body feel? Heavy or anxious? Light or calm? Does the worry or sensation grow or expand?

Now focus your attention on something lovely or someone you love. Notice something beautiful or for which you are grateful. Put your hand on your heart and breathe in the love or gratitude. Now how do you feel?

Your body absorbs the focal attention of your mind. Put your attention, one at a time, on five gifts of love around you and open your heart to fully absorb the depth of that love. As you notice, put your hand on your open heart and say, "Thank you Love/God, for loving me with this gift of _____!"

#7

Making Space for Balance and Rest

*D*on't you think it's time you let yourself rest? You've spent most of your life trying, believing there's somewhere you need to get to or something you should be doing to get somewhere. And yet, I am here with you now, in this moment, inviting you to just stop for a while and be with Me. Stop and let down. Stop and feel My breath, breathing with you. Stop and feel the bliss of our union. You've been away so long, and I've missed your presence. I know it's difficult for you to be still enough to let your mind rest. For even sitting still, you are often far away in thought, never even realizing how close you are to Me and how much I long to have you notice and feel My nearness. You've trained your mind for too long to the illusions of this world. It takes only a little willingness to see beyond this veil. ~Love Itself

**Draw the outline of a gingerbread man in the center of a blank page. Within it, place your name. On the top half of the page, write the activities you've done in the past week that have been energizing or restorative to you. Draw arrows toward your figure indicating the nourishment and energy they have given to you. Then, on the bottom half of the page, write the activities or emotional stressors/worries that have occurred for you in the past week that

have taken your energy. Draw arrows away from your figure indicating the energy they have taken.

Next, sit back and reflect upon what you might do differently or release to allow Divine Love to manage the energy drainers. What could you fully surrender and entrust to Divine Love? You might put a big "S" for surrender through each of these. Note what you might do that would require less effort and stress on your part. Consider what you might add to the top that would recharge and restore you. Add these thoughts and reflections to your picture. Change the image and activities to create a more peaceful, balanced you. Color as you like!

....

* * *

ABOUT THE AUTHOR

Janine is a Licensed Professional Clinical Counselor and Counseling Supervisor in Upper Sandusky, OH. She has spent the last 30 plus years meeting and joining individuals from every walk of life as they journey through their life struggles, overcome obstacles, and discover their inner power. Through her private counseling & life coaching practice, retreats, workshops, and public speaking engagements, Janine has spent her career joining individuals on their healing journey. She has helped each not only heal through trauma, loss, and degradation of the soul but more so awaken to their innate worth and power as they come to recognize the Divine Light within themselves. She has made it her mission to bring spiritual depth and awareness to the healing process of therapy. Janine resides in Upper Sandusky, Ohio with her husband, Jere, and two beagles, Mazzie and Lillie.

Made in the USA
Middletown, DE
28 July 2022

70135958R10149